THE ECONOMIC FOUNDATIONS OF INTELLIGENT INVESTING

Volume II • Microeconomics

Fourth Edition

Panos Mourdoukoutas

Cover Image: Can Stock Photo Inc./

Acknowledgment:

p. 60: Table entitled "The *Business Week* Top Twenty-Five Innovative Firms in 2008" appeared in *Business Week* online, April 24, 2006. Copyright © 2006 by Business Week. Reprinted by permission of Business Week via the Copyright Clearance Center.

4750 Venture Drive, Suite 400
Ann Arbor, MI 48108
800-562-2147

To my family

CONTENTS

LIST OF EXHIBITS

PREFACE

INTELLIGENT INVESTING BEGINS WITH SOUND ECONOMICS

"Crisis breeds opportunity," so goes the old proverb. When banks were failing one after another in 1991, investors were indiscriminately selling every bank stock. This sort of behavior presented a golden opportunity for prudent investors to pick up good stocks thrown away together with bad stocks. One of these stocks was Citibank, which investors could pick up at $10 a share and sell for $200 five years later.

When the high-tech bubble burst in 2002, investors indiscriminately sold every technology stock. This sort of behavior presented an opportunity for prudent investors to grab promising high-tech companies at a deep discount. New York-based Corning, Inc. is a case in point. Its stock price dropped from around $95 in early 2001 to around $2 in late 2002! By 2005, the company's stock rebounded to $25, handsomely rewarding those who bought it at $2.

Citibank and Corning aren't the only companies that have managed to survive financial crises and thrive, rewarding their stockholders. P&G, Coca Cola, McDonald's, Amgen, Microsoft, and Walmart have experienced phenomenal equity appreciation. At the same time, a number of other companies like LA Gear, Kmart, Nortel Networks, Global Crossing, and MCI-Wordcom have either filed for bankruptcy or barely escaped it, seeing their stock plummet. Why do some companies survive and thrive, while others decline and fail? What makes the difference?

A sound business strategy lets these companies achieve sustainable competitive advantage—above industry average rates of return over a long period of time. Corning's business strategy, for instance, is based on innovation. Over its 160 year history, the company has churned off scores of innovative products, from glass for Thomas Edison's light bulb, to glass for rockets, kitchenware, and telescopes. Coca-Cola and Nike focused on branding and mass-merchandising. McDonald's pioneered and perfected franchising. Walmart mastered economies of scale. Microsoft mastered the economies of networking.

The difference between winning and losing stocks is the soundness or nonsoundness of the business strategies of the underlying companies, and the understanding of the economic concepts behind these strategies. Sound portfolio management should begin with the strategy of the publicly listed companies and the ability of their leadership to gain and preserve a competitive edge against their peers by effectively applying a number of microeconomic concepts and principles, the subject of this volume.

ACKNOWLEDGMENT

The author is thankful to Parvez Hussain for his assistance with the preparation of some of the exhibits in this book.

INTRODUCTION
ECONOMIC CONCEPTS BEHIND SUCCESSFUL INVESTMENT STRATEGY

Everyone who closely follows the performance of equity markets cannot help but get dizzy with their erratic and volatile performance. Up one moment, down the next moment, up one day, down the next, up one month, down the next, up one year, down the next, and so on. Some people, called "traders," try to take advantage of this erratic behavior of financial markets, by timing the market, "buy low" and "sell high (long-buying)," or "sell high" and "buy-back low" (short-selling). Others, called "investors," try to spot trends out of these erratic patterns—betting on stocks with an upward trend, and taking bets off the table for stocks with downward patterns. Which strategy works? Can traders and investors "time" the market? Can investors and traders buy and sell the right stocks at the right time?

Economists and financial analysts are divided into three schools on these questions. The first school follows the "efficiency hypothesis theory," arguing that markets always discount public information, that is, stock prices always reflect whatever information is available. This means that prospective traders and investors cannot take advantage of stock price moves. If company XYZ announces an increase in its profit Monday morning at 9 a.m., the stock will open sharply higher at 9:30 a.m. Investors who chase after the stock may end up losing rather than making money, selling the stock of company KLM to buy the stock of company XYZ may end up losing money on both trades. That's why "efficiency hypothesis" theorists suggest investors and traders should avoid trying to time the market, switching from one stock to another and invest in "Index Funds," investment vehicles that allow their holders to participate in the appreciation of a popular index. "S&P Spiders," for instance, is a product that allows investors to participate in the appreciation of the S&P 500 (an average that monitors the price of 500 stocks trading on the New York Stock Exchange).

The second school of investment follows "technical analysis," a method that relies on daily, weekly, monthly, and annual charts of stock prices and trading volumes to identify patterns and trends. When the stock price of a company, for instance, breaks the upper bound of a "trading range" with an unusually large volume, it signals an upward trend; it is time to buy and hold. Conversely, when the stock price of a company breaks below the lower bound of a range with an unusually large volume, it signals a downward trend; it is time to sell and stay away. Likewise, a "head and shoulders" chart is bearish, while a "reverse head and shoulders" chart is bullish.

The third school of investment follows the "fundamental analysis," applying a set of economic and financial indicators to separate the winners from the losers. One such indicator is profit margin, e.g., profit over the cost of sales. Rising profit margins are bullish, while declining profit margins are bearish for the stocks of the underlying companies. Another indicator is market share, the percent of industry sales dominated by different companies. The largest the market share of the company, the better the company is positioned to take advantage of "economies of scale," the cost savings associated with a larger production size—a bullish sign. A third indicator is a company's pricing power, e.g., its ability to raise prices, maintaining and expanding profit margins; the better positioned a company to raise prices, the higher its profit margins—a bullish sign. A fourth indicator is the company's ability to innovate, that is, to discover and exploit new market opportunities, develop new business models, churn out new products and processes. Innovative companies experience explosive growth and robust equity performance, and so on. A fifth indicator is a company's ability to create a network of users for its products. Companies with a large network of users set the standards for their industry, creating and preserving sustainable competitive advantages that boost profitability and equity prices.

Among the followers of this school are legendary investors Benjamin Graham and Warren Buffett. Benjamin Graham applied fundamental analysis in the 1930s to identify stocks that had been unfairly punished in the sell-off of the Great Depression. His strategy was to buy the stock of companies with a strong balance sheet selling at half their cash value. Warren Buffett applied fundamental analysis in the 1960s to identify companies with a unique market position, which allowed them to enjoy rising profit margins overtime. Coca Cola, McDonald's, Wrigley, Moody's, and P&G are some of the companies that fit this profile and are therefore included in Buffett's portfolio. Which school is right? Which method of investing yields better investment choices?

Each investment method has its merits and demerits, depending on the "context," the conditions and circumstances of financial markets at different places and times, as well as the objectives and constraints of market participants. In an uptrend ("bullish") market, associated with a growing economy, the efficiency school approach to investing is most likely to yield superior results to the other two strategies, as it saves investors the time, the transaction fees, and often the taxes associated with "active" portfolio management. In a downtrend ("bearish") or sideways market, associated with a declining economy, the technical and the fundamental analysis approach are most likely to yield superior results. This means that investors must be flexible with the strategy they adopt, always evaluating the conditions and the circumstances that affect their portfolio of companies, always appraising the performance of each and every company they consider buying, holding, or selling.

To perform this task, investors need to be well versed in certain principles and concepts of economics. To evaluate the "big context," the economy-wide conditions, investors must understand macroeconomics, especially the business cycle and the ways it affects different asset classes and different industries—the subject of the first volume of this book. To evaluate the "small context," the industry-wide conditions and the performance of individual firms, investors must understand microeconomics—the subject of the second volume of this book.

Microeconomics provides investors with the concepts and theories that help companies develop sustainable competitive advantage—above average net profit and equity performance over the long-term—by raising revenues and cutting expenses:

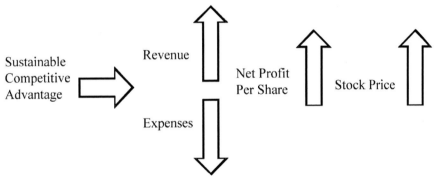

"Economies of scale," for instance, have helped Walmart cut its expenses and expand its revenues, achieving consistent earnings growth that translated to a 100% gain over the period 1998–2008. Economies of scope have allowed P&G to achieve 120% over the same period, while innovation allowed Apple's stock to soar by 1500% (See Exhibit 0.1), handsomely rewarding its stockholders with a stellar equity performance, and most notably Walmart's founder Sam Walton. Economies of networking allowed Microsoft to dominate the computer software industry and eBay online auctions; innovation allowed Corning to dominate the glass substance industry, surviving and thriving in its 160-year history; branding helped P&G dominate the consumer staples market and Nike the shoe segment of the apparel industry; franchising allowed McDonald's to dominate the fast food industries.

Exhibit 0.1

Sustainable Competitive Advantage and Equity Performance for Selected Companies

Company	Source of Advantage	Performance (%)*
Walmart	Economies of Scale	100
P&G	Economies of Scope	120
Microsoft	Economies of Networking	60
Apple	Innovation	1500
Corning	Innovation	1400**
Qualcomm	Innovation	2000
Nike	Branding	500
Coca Cola	Branding	100
McDonald's	Branding/Franchising	320
Wrigley	Branding	150

* Stock appreciation over a ten-year period (1998–2008).
** 2001–2007.

These concepts aren't independent the one from another. Economies of scale support and reinforce branding, while branding supports and reinforces economies of scale. Coke's large presence in the soft drink market supports and reinforces its brand, while its strong brand allows Coke to expand its scale. Networking supports and reinforces scale, while scale supports and reinforces networking. Innovation supports and reinforces branding; economies of networking support and reinforce franchising. Apple's strong innovation supports its brand; and McDonald's network economies supports its franchising.

In short, portfolio selection begins with business strategy—the microeconomic concepts and theories that allow companies to develop sustainable competitive advantage—that translates to high profitability—the ultimate source of robust equity performance.

Applying the right microeconomic concepts and theories doesn't necessary lead to sustainable competitive advantage, however. A large scale or a good brand name, for instance, doesn't automatically translate into a sustainable competitive advantage. General Motors and Kmart were both large companies with a strong brand name, but they eventually filed for bankruptcy. This means that identifying companies that have sustainable competitive advantage requires the crunching of industry and company statistics that connect microeconomic concepts with performance, such as rising revenue growth, rising market shares, pricing power, rising profit margins, and economic profit:

Rising Revenue Growth

Rising revenue growth implies a robust demand for the company' products, allowing the company to achieve economies of scale and the cost savings associated with it. Rising sales further allows the company to plow some of its revenues to R&D and advertising further strengthening its position. Apple, for instance, has managed to consistently raise its sales by introducing new products. Kraft Foods, Heinz, and General Mills have also managed to expand sales by introducing new products. Chipotle Restaurants has managed to raise sales by opening more Mexican-style restaurants in the U.S. while Yum Brands has managed to expand sales by opening up more Pizza-Hut and Kentucky Fried chicken stores in China.

Rising Market Shares

Market share is the portion of a market controlled by a company. Rising market shares imply that the company gains market power vis-à-vis its competitors, preserving its scale or brand advantage. Apple and Google, for instance, have managed to gain market power and advantage over Research in Motion by gaining market share.

Rising Pricing Power

Pricing power is the ability of a company to maintain or even raise the prices of its products without losing customers to competition. Pricing power is associated with the existence of little competition for the company's products, that is, the existence of few substitutes for the company's products. This is usually the case for companies that enjoy a near monopoly situation, such as utilities, railroads, pharmaceuticals, and bond grading agencies.

Rising Profit Margins

Profit margin is the markup a company enjoys over sales costs. Rising profit margins mean that the company executes its strategy effectively. It translates whatever is the source of its advantage into profit.

Crunching company statistics for public companies listed in major exchanges isn't as complicated as it sounds. Most of the above statistics are provided in corporate reports and in financial sites, like yahoo.finance.com. Research in Motion's financial statistics, for instance, can be found in this site under the entry "key statistics," (see Exhibit 0.2), while comparisons with competitors can be found under the entry "competitors." (See Exhibit 0.3). While the revenues and profit margins of Research in Motion have been growing faster than those of Nokia, they lag behind of those of Apple which can explain the relative stock price performance of the three stocks (see Exhibit 0.4 and Exhibit 05).

Exhibit 0.2

Apple Key Statistics in April of 2011

	Apple	Research in Motion	Nokia
Revenue (ttm)	$87.45B	19.91B	64B
Quarterly Revenue Growth (yoy)	82.70%	36.20%	9.20
Operating Profit Margin	29.02%	23.80%	5.13
Gross Profit	$25.68B	8.82B	17.20
Quarterly Earnings Growth	94.80%	31.60	-1.40
P/E	12.35	6.50	12.01

Source: Finance.yahoo.com.

Exhibit 0.3

Relative Stock Performance:
Apple versus Research in Motion

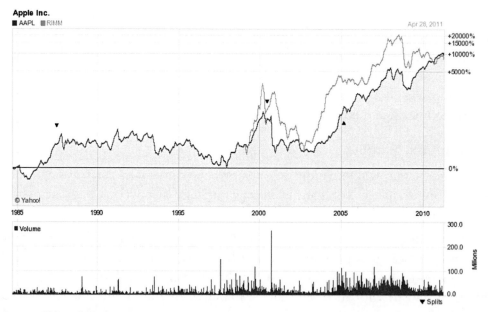

Source: Yahoo.finance.com.

Exhibit 0.4

Relative Stock Performance:
Apple versus Nokia

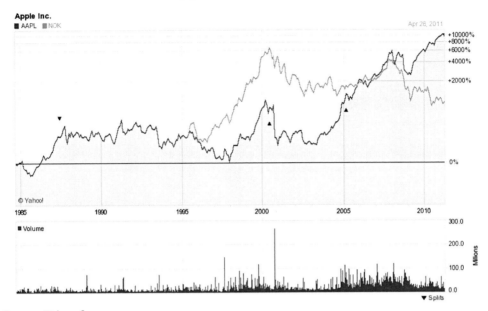

Source: Yahoo.finance.com.

Exhibit 0.5

Apple Key Statistics in May of 2021

	Apple	Research in Motion (BlackBerry	Nokia
Revenue (ttm)	$325.45B	4.83B	22B
Quarterly Revenue Growth (yoy)	53.60%	-25.30%	3.30
Operating Profit Margin	27.32%	-10.75%	5.13
Gross Profit	$104.96B	643M	8.59
Quarterly Earnings Growth	110.10%	–	–
P/E	28.05	–	16.86

Source: Finance.yahoo.com.

Economic Profit

Economic profit is the difference between return on invested capital (ROIC) and weighted average cost of capital (WACC).

Economic profit is also a measure of a company's competitive advantage. A rising economic profit indicates that a company's advantage is strengthening, while a declining economic profit indicates that a company's competitive advantage is eroding. Home Depot's competitive advantage, for instance, has been strengthening, as its economic profit has been rising, while GameStop's advantage has been weakening (Exhibit 0.6 and Exhibit 0.7).

Exhibit 0.6

Home Depot's Economic Profit

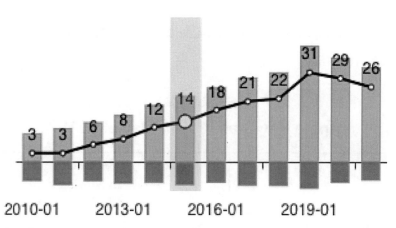

Source: Gurufocus, May, 22, 2021.

Exhibit 0.7

GameStop's Advantage Has been Declining

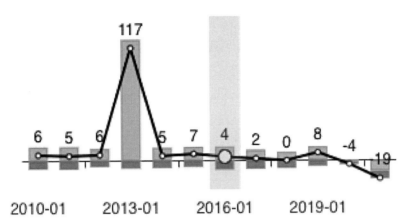

Source: Gurufocus, May, 22, 2021.

Peter Lynch's Method of Picking up Winning Stocks

Peter Lynch was the manager of Fidelity's Magellan fund between 1977 and 1990, which averaged a 29.2% annual return, consistently more than double the S&P 500 stock market index and making it the best-performing mutual fund in the world during that period.

Here are some of the principles of Peter Lynch's investment style.

- Begin with a list of companies you like as a consumer. Consumers are at the center of the market universe, the beginning and the ending of everything companies do. Companies that are popular with consumers usually make good investments. They make a lot of profit, which translates into price gains for their shares, e.g., Starbucks, Netflix, and Costco.

But not all popular companies make good investments, not all popular companies deliver a great deal of profits, which leads to the next step.

- Determine which companies have sustainable competitive advantage, make returns on the invested capital that exceed the cost of raising that capital (positive economic profit) over a long period of time that is.

One way to determine sustainable competitive advantage is to analyze the Strengths, the Weaknesses, the Opportunities, and the Threats of the different companies (SWOT analysis).

Usual Strengths—Sources of Competitive Advantage

- Leadership and management (Google, Amazon, Tesla)
- Economies of scale and scope (Walmart, Pfizer)
- Economies of networking (Microsoft, eBay, Amazon, Booking.com, Facebook)
- Branding (Nike, Adidas, Apple)
- Franchising (McDonald's, Starbucks, Yum Brands)
- Bundling (Verizon, AT&T)
- Innovation (Apple, Amazon)

Usual Weakness

- Too much dependence on a few major customers—defense contractors
- Too much dependence on a few suppliers—semiconductor makers
- Too sensitive to business cycles—automobile and appliance makers
- Too sensitive to political environment—defense contractors
- Too expensive to reproduce its competitive advantage—airline companies, computer hardware makers
- Lack of pricing power—Uber and Lyft

Opportunities

- New resource and commodity markets
- New ways of shipping and distribution
- New products
- New processes
- New business models

Usual Threats

- Imitation
- Alternative products
- Market saturation

Application

Costco: Great Company, Great Investment

The microeconomic concepts and theories behind successful business and investment strategies are explained in more detail in the following eight chapters. The first chapter explains the concept of "economies of scale," and the ways it has contributed the success of retailers like Walmart, Costco, and Target. The second chapter discusses the concept of "economies of scope," and its contribution to the success of consumer staples companies like Procter & Gamble, Kraft, Nestle, and Colgate Palmolive. The third chapter discusses the concept of "branding" and its contribution to the competitive advantages of companies like Coca Cola, Pepsi, and Nike, Inc. The fourth chapter focuses on the concept of bundling, and its importance for the success of restaurant chains like Pizza Hut and Kentucky Fried Chicken owned by Yum! Brands. The fifth chapter discusses the economies of networking and its contribution to the success of companies like Microsoft and eBay, Inc. The sixth chapter is a discussion of "franchising" and its contribution to the sustainable competitive advantage of companies like McDonald's. The seventh chapter discusses the concept of innovation and its contribution to the success of companies like Apple, IBM, and Corning, Inc. The eighth chapter summarizes and concludes the discussion.

Source: Gurufocus, November 20, 2020.

Additional Reading

"5 Key Takeaways From Warren Buffett's 2021 Letter" Gurufocus Feb 28 2021.

Warren Buffett's (Trades, Portfolio) annual letter to Berkshire Hathaway (BRK.A)(BRK.B) shareholders offers great wisdom to value investors, and this year is no exception to this rule. The highly successful value investor released his 2021 letter on Saturday. Here are my five top takeaways from the letter

1. Focus on operating earnings

Operating earnings are the most accurate representation of a company's performance. "Operating earnings are what count most, even during periods when they are not the largest item in our GAAP total," Buffett wrote. The legendary investor has been critical of companies using broader performance measures like EBITDA, which doesn't count for all business expenses.

2. Don't underestimate the power of retained earnings

Retained earnings are the "magic" that makes millions for shareholders in the long-term. "What's out of sight, however, should not be out of mind: Those unrecorded retained earnings are usually building value—lots of value—for Berkshire," wrote Buffett. "Investees use the withheld funds to expand their business, make acquisitions, pay off debt and, often, to repurchase their stock (an act that increases our share of their future earnings)."

3. Invest in businesses with good economic characteristics and good managers

"It took me a while to wise up," he explained. "But Charlie—and also my 20-year struggle with the textile operation I inherited at Berkshire—finally convinced me that owning a non-controlling portion of a wonderful business is more profitable, more enjoyable, and far less work than struggling with 100% of a marginal enterprise."

4. Use common sense to look at a company's competitive strengths and core capabilities

"Simply deploy your capital into whatever we believe makes the most sense, based on a company's durable competitive strengths, the capabilities and character of its management, and price," he wrote. "If that strategy requires little or no effort on our part, so much the better."

5. Don't overpay for what you buy

The legendary investor has often been quoted that "price is what you pay value is what you get." Paying more than the intrinsic value leaves no room for error and may result in losses that undermine portfolio performance.

That's what happened with one of the investments Buffett made back in 2016 when he purchased Precision Castparts ("PCC"), which resulted in an $11 billion write-down. "No one misled me in any way—I was simply too optimistic about PCC's normalized profit potential," he explains. "Last year, my miscalculation was laid bare by adverse developments throughout the aerospace industry, PCC's most important source of customers."

Review Questions

1. Can investors "time" the market?

2. Which investment school does Warren Buffett follow?

3. What is sustainable competitive advantage? How can in be attained?

4. What is the relationship between sustainable competitive advantage and equity performance?

5. What is the relationship between microeconomics and sound investment strategy?

6. What makes a good company a good investment? Give examples

Chapter One

ECONOMIES OF SCALE

Can large retail stores succeed in less densely populated rural areas? Yes, if located in the right place that serves the surrounding communities. That's Sam Walton's idea that turned his rural Walton's Five and Dime general merchandise store in Bentonville, Arkansas (a town of 2,900 people) into Walmart, the world's largest retail chain. By 2008, Walmart had thousands of stores all over the world, generating $400 billion in sales, and $92 billion in gross profits.

The company's startling success has drawn the attention of Wall Street, and most notably, institutional investors who have been rushing to include Walmart in their portfolios. The company's stock rose from a few dollars in early 1970, when it went public, to $540 (adjusted for splits) by 2008!

Walmart's success can be attributed to the mastering and executing of a very well-known concept in economics, economies of scale, and the technological know-how of its founder Sam Walton that supports and reinforces it and its successors.

What Is It?

Economies of scale are the cost savings associated with a larger *production* scale (size) of a certain product; the larger the production scale, the lower the *per unit* (average) product cost. (See Exhibit 1.1) Manufacturing 1,000 laptops is cheaper than manufacturing 100 laptops. This means that economies of scale arise on the supply side of the market, on savings from a larger production batch with the same fixed resources, on gains from improved bargaining power with suppliers, on better use of logistics, etc.

Economies of scale are more evident in industries that require large fixed costs, which spread as production size expands. Economies of scale, for instance, are present in the electric industry, which requires large fixed outlays for the building of power generating factories and the wiring of neighborhoods; the cable TV industry, which must also wire the neighborhoods and provide content; the manufacturing industries that require the setting up of assembly lines and large distribution networks; the retailing that requires the leasing of large retail space; and the franchising industry, which requires large expenses in developing and promoting the product and business concept.

Exhibit 1.1

Economies of Scale Are Associated with Falling Costs

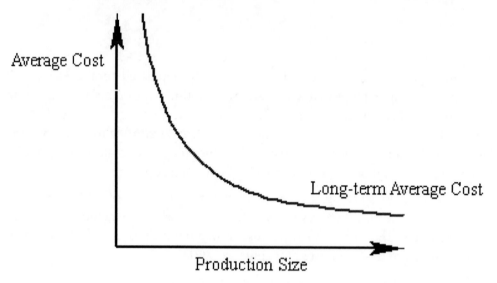

It comes as no surprise, therefore, that the world's largest corporations are in these industries (see Exhibit 1.2).

Why Is It Important?

Economies of scale contribute to corporate profitability and superior equity performance in a number of ways. First, they allow companies to overcome the "Law of Diminishing Marginal Productivity," the declining productivity when successive units of labor are added to the existing production facilities—due to overcrowding of labor vis-à-vis the production facilities. Second, they allow companies to raise output faster than economic resources, raising productivity and cutting unit costs. In the late nineteenth century, Andrew Carnegie improved efficiency by mass-producing steel, cutting steel production costs and lowering steel prices. Economies of scale allowed Standard Oil Corporation to cut kerosene production costs from 2.5 cents in 1879 to 0.4 cents by 1885. Mass production allowed German chemical producers BASF, Bayer, and Hoechst to cut the price of Alizarin from DM200 per kilogram in 1878 to DM9 by 1886, underselling foreign competitors. In the early twentieth-century automobile industry, Henry Ford improved efficiency by mass-producing, mass-distributing, and mass-advertising the Model T car, cutting car prices from $850 in 1908 to $360 by 1916. In the late twentieth century retail industry Walmart improved efficiency with large retail outlets and volume sales, which again translated to lower costs and lower prices for consumers. Economies of scale allowed Texas Instruments to mass produce pocket calculators; Panasonic, Sharp, and Samsung to mass-produce microwave ovens; IBM portable computers; Gillette disposable razors; and Black and Decker food processors.

Third, economies of scale allow corporations to raise their market share, which helps them improve their bargaining power with suppliers. Fourth, they allow companies to cut costs for new products and reach what marketers call the "early majority," a large group of price sensitive consumers, as observed in the diffusion of new durable products, whereby demand begins with a small group of consumers understanding the merits of adoption, and spreads them to larger and larger groups until it reaches a cascade. The widespread use of disposable diapers is a case in point. In 1956, disposable diaper adoption rate was only 1%, as they cost 9 cents per unit and their performance was poor, due to leakage. Ten years later, disposable diapers cost 5.5 cents while their performance improved substantially. The diaper market exploded, from $10 million in 1966 to $370 billion in 1973, with P&G dominating it.[1]

Exhibit 1.2

The Fortune Twenty-Five Largest Firms in 2021

1. Walmart	6. Berkshire Hathaway
2. Amazon	7. United Health Group
3. Exxon Mobil	8. McKesson
4. Apple	9. AT&T
5. CVS Health	10. AmerisourceBergen

Source: *Fortune Magazine.*

How Are They Attained?

Economies of scale can be attained in two ways. First, internally or organically, though the expansion of the existing facilities. Banks can expand their production scale by opening new branches in different locations. Bakeries can expand their production capabilities by bringing down their walls and building bigger oven facilities, and by setting up new retail outlets. Retailers can expand their scale of operations by opening new outlets with the same or different brand names catered to different market segments. Walmart, for instance, has been expanding the scale of its operations, both by opening up new stores and by setting up stores with different names, such as Sam's Club, that allowed the company to expand into consumer-membership market. Home Depot has been expanding by opening up new stores and by setting up a subsidiary that caters to the home-remodeling market.

Companies can further expand internally through the introduction of new technologies. Intel, for instance, has for years managed to cut the costs of its microprocessors by shifting production to larger manufacturing facilities. In 2003, the company shifted production from 200mm (8-inch) wafer manufacturing facilities to 300mm (12-inch) wafers, churning more than twice as many equivalent chips per wafer as 200 mm wafers."[2] Corning has managed to cut its flat panel production costs by the introduction of large generation substrates that allow for the manufacturing of larger and a greater number of panels from each substrate.[3] The introduction of new technology has allowed leading flat panel TV manufacturer Sharp to enjoy higher productivity and higher profit margins. For the period 1999–2004, Sharp enjoyed close to 5% profit margin, twice that of Sony, and about three times that of Matsushita.[4] In 2005, Hitachi introduced a new storage disk that allowed desktop PCs to store a trillion bytes, twice as many as current models, cutting storage costs in half. The introduction of two new technologies, Platinum Multicast and FLO (Forward Link Only), by Qualcomm allowed the company to cut the multimedia content delivery over cellular devices.[5]

Second, economies of scale can be attained externally, through mergers and acquisitions (M&A) and through partnerships, strategic alliances, and joint ventures. In the retail sector, Walmart's acquisition of Mohr-Value stores in 1977, for instance, allowed the company to quickly expand to Michigan and Illinois; its acquisition of Kuhn's Big K in the early 1980s accommodated the company's rapid entry into Southern states; and its acquisition of Woolco stores in 1994 allowed it to expand into Canada. In the energy sector, Calpine's $576 billion acquisition of SkyGen Energy LLC and Panda Energy International in 2000 boosted the company's capacity by 60% by the year 2004. Devon Energy Corporation's $3.4 billion acquisition of Anderson Exploration, Inc. turned Devon to the largest oil and gas producer in North America. In the steel industry, Nucor's stream of acquisitions in the late 1990s and the early 2000s gave the company a cost edge against its competitors.[6] In the computer hardware sector, the merger of Compaq with Hewlett-Packard allowed the two companies to eliminate a number of product duplications including the HP Jornada and Omnibook, and Compaq's Itanium-based servers, saving the new company $0.9 billion in sales costs, $1.6 billion in operating expenses, and $0.5 billion in R&D costs.[7] In forklift manufacturing, Toyota's acquisition of BT Industries allowed the company to cut the distribution and sales costs of its forklift trucks.

In the late nineteenth century oil industry, Standard Oil expanded the scale of the company's operations by acquiring competitors or driving them out of business, as did American Tobacco, United Fruit, U.S. Steel, International Harvester, and GE. In the first quarter of the twentieth century, William C. Durrant expanded the product offerings of GM by merging twenty-five smaller automobile companies, including Buick, with Oldsmobile and Cadillac to create a larger company. Swift's expansion to meat distribution allowed the company to set its prices 75 cents below the competition.

Economies of scale can be also achieved through alliances and joint partnerships, where two or more companies, often former competitors, pull their resources together to mass produce a product, while maintaining their independence. Automobile makers like Daimler Chrysler, for instance, have teamed up with Mitsubishi and Hyundai to develop the first family of world engines to power as many as one million small vehicles. Ford Motor Company has teamed up with Mazda Motor Corp to develop an engine for their cars as well as cars produced by Volvo. The alliance between Renault and Nissan saved the two companies $3.3 billion in the areas of purchasing and product development. The External Equipment Provider alliance allowed member companies like Dow Corning, Nordson Company, and DEK to improve productivity and cut costs by standardizing their materials, equipment, and procurement. The co-production alliance between flash memory chipmakers SanDisk, Toshiba, and Hitachi allowed the three companies to cut costs for digital camera chips. The FreeMove, an alliance among major European mobile service providers Orange, Telefonica, T Mobile, and TIM allowed these companies to expand the scale of their operations, reaching 170 million customers. Fourth, international business can achieve economies of scale by forming consortia that allow global units to amass the critical mass to enter overseas markets. New Zealand's EE Group, a consortium of thirty firms, got a project to build 40,000 apartments in Turkey.[8]

Economies of scale are an efficient and effective way of gaining competitive advantage by cutting cost through scale, which can be achieved internally through the replication of company facilities and the introduction of new technology, and externally through M&A, strategic alliances, and joint ventures and partnerships. Each of these methods has its own limitations. Internal expansion is slow but better controlled. External expansion is fast, but hard to control and reconcile, especially for technology companies with different software platforms and corporate cultures.

Tips for Investors—Be Selective—Scale Doesn't Always Translate to Higher Profits and Equity Prices

The concept of economies of scale applies to the production of a single product or family of homogeneous products that cater to the same market, but even in these cases, it has an important limitation: the growing bureaucracy associated with larger organizations and the inability to adjust to rapidly changing market conditions. Some large and diverse companies experience diseconomies rather than economies of scale. Other companies deploy economies of scale to benefit their management and unionized labor rather than stockholders, as has been the case with GM, which has seen its stock declining steadily since the 1950s, trading at around $2 in the early 2009, shortly before the company filed for bankruptcy!

In industries conducive to scale, investors should buy the largest player with rising market shares and profit margins, like Walmart in consumer staples, Home Depot in building materials, Staples in office supplies, and Toyota Motor Company in the automobile industry; and avoid companies with declining market shares and profit margins, like General Motors. Investors should further keep a wary eye to challengers. Walmart Stores has been seriously challenged by Target.

Summary

Economies of scale are the cost savings associated with a larger *production* scale of a *certain* product; the larger the production scale, the lower the per unit product cost. Economies of scale contribute to corporate profitability and superior equity performance. Economies of scale are more evident in industries that require large fixed costs, which spread as production size expands, such as the electric, the telecommunications, and the cable service industries. Economies of scale can be achieved both internally by expanding existing operations and externally through mergers and acquisitions and strategic alliances. A larger scale doesn't always translate to superior corporate performance. For every Walmart Stores there is a Kmart, and for every Toyota, there is a GM.

Application
Right Size, Wrong Leadership

Hewlett Packard, Bank of America, and General Motors are in different businesses, but they do have two things in common: The first thing is a large corporate scale. Hewlett-Packard ranks 31 in this year's *Fortune's* list of 500 largest global firms; Bank of America 46; and General Motors 17. The second thing is a poor equity performance. Over the last five years, Hewlett-Packard's stock lost 58% of its value, Bank of America's stock 85%, and GM's stock 45%.

Economists argue that large corporations usually have a cost advantage over their smaller peers, which translates to higher profits and stock prices, as has been the case with other large corporations that made the Fortune Global 500 list. Walmart and Apple, for instance, have gained 50% and 300% respectively, over the same period. What can explain this disconnect between corporate size and corporate performance?

Company	Fortune 2012 Company Global Rank	Five-year Return on Equity
Hewlett-Packard	31	-58%
General Electric(NYSE:GE)	22	-45
General Motors	17	-45
Citigroup (NYSE:C)	60	-90
Bank of America	46	-85
Toyota Motor Company (NYSE:TM)	10	-38
S&P 500		-10

Certainly, each of these corporations has its own specific problems that make it difficult to come up with a single answer to this question, but they all spring from one factor: the wrong leadership. Hewlett-Packard's leadership, for instance, embarked on a string of acquisitions that grew the company in the wrong direction, in declining and highly competitive segments of the high technology industry. Bank of America purchased the wrong companies at the wrong time. Toyota's leadership failed to deal effectively with a stronger yen and quality issues for some of its models, as well as the competition from Korean automakers. GM's leadership turned the company into a welfare agency for the benefit of its management and unionized labor rather than stockholders.

Source: *Forbes Magazine.*

Application
Best Buy's Two Key Advantages in Fighting Amazon

Big-box retailer Best Buy Co., Inc. is still in business, standing up to Amazon. com Inc., and thriving.

Last week, the company said its enterprise comparable sales increased 23% from last year amidst a 174% jump in online sales that fueled stronger than expected third-quarter earnings.

Over the past three years, Best Buy's sales increased 10%, while its EBITDA rose 10.7%.

Company	Best Buy	Walmart	Amazon
3-year Revenue Growth (%)	10	5.4	25.6
3-year EBITDA Growth (%)	10.7	3.6	42.2
Current Operating Margin (%)	4.96	3.93	5.72
Average Annual Total Return (2010–20)	13.07	13.71	34.75
Market Price	$113.90	$150.4	$3,142.4
Intrinsic Value	$82.18	$115.41	$2,835.4

Company	ROIC %	WACC %	ROIC-WACC % (Economic profit)
Best Buy	18.21	11.28	6.93
Walmart	8.73	3.39	5.34
Amazon	11.37	9.48	1.89

In a statement, CEO Corie Barry praised the company's "strong quarterly results in the midst of unprecedented times."

"Our comparable sales grew a remarkable 23% as we leveraged our unique capabilities, including our supply chain expertise, flexible store operating model and ability to shift quickly to digital, to meet what is clearly elevated demand for products that help customers work, learn, cook, entertain and connect in their homes," Barry added. "The current environment has underscored our purpose to enrich lives through technology, and the capabilities we are flexing and strengthening now will benefit us going forward as we execute our strategy."

Barry also noted Best Buy's employees "showed empathy, ingenuity and extraordinary execution throughout the quarter," which is reflected in its economic profit at 6.93% above those of Walmart, Inc. (WMT, Financial) and Amazon.

That's a big turnaround from more than a decade ago when Amazon's arrival in the big-box retail space changed the game. Best Buy's most important asset location and scale turned into liabilities. In what has come to be known as "show-rooming," customers did their window-shopping at Best Buy and their actual shopping at Amazon.com which offered better deals.

Best Buy's revenue, profits and stock headed south, causing business strategists and stock analysts to predict the slow decline of the company.

But it didn't happen. Best Buy survived and thrived, delivering an average annual total return of 13.07% between 2010 and 2020.

What's driving Best Buy's survival? A smart strategy Renew Blue launched six years ago, which changed the game.

Renew Blue helped Best Buy capitalize on the benefits of scale and location—in several ways. One of them was the introduction of a matching prices policy. This was accommodated by a push in certain states to have online retailers collect taxes, narrowing the gap between online and in-store sales.

And then there's the benefit of using stores as warehouses and pick-up places to speed up online order delivery.

There's also the expansion of product offerings in each store location to catch up with emerging consumer electronics trends like home theaters and computing, health technology solutions and assured living. The concept of stores within stores was also implemented, with Korean electronics giant Samsung (XKRX:005930, Financial) and Microsoft (MSFT, Financial) opening up in Best Buy stores. In essence, the company shifted the cost of show-rooming to these manufacturers.

The rest is history. Samsung and Microsoft were followed by Alphabet's (GOOG, Financial) (GOOGL, Financial) Google, turning the partnership between Best Buy and electronics vendors into a form of collective entrepreneurship that benefited both parties.

Meanwhile, the company continues to gain the synergies associated with increased customer traffic and the efficient and effective deployment of its Geek Squad to customers who buy flat-screen TVs and other accessories that need installation services.

In short, Best Buy's turnaround is the result of a deliberate strategy that allowed the company to leverage its key assets, scale and location to ride a new retailing trend, the merger of online and offline sales—a policy similar to that pursued by other brick-and-mortar retailers.

Disclosure: I own shares of Amazon.

Source: Gurufocus, December, 1, 2020.

Review Questions

1. What are returns to scale?
2. Why are they important for corporate profitability and equity performance?
3. How are economies of scale attained?
4. Do economies of scale always translate to higher equity prices?
5. Which industries are most conducive to economies of scale?
6. How do economies of scale contribute to a company's sustainable competitive advantage?
7. What are the limitations of this strategy?

Investment Link

Find the following information for Walmart Stores:

Current Stock Price

Core Business

Major Competitors

Sales

Revenue

Cost of Sales

Gross Profit

Net Profit

Profit Margin

Notes

1. Markides, Costas and Paul Geroski (2004), 4.

2. 2003 Annual Report, Santa Clara, California, 8.

3. 2004 Annual Report and 2005 Proxy Statement, 60.

4. Einborn, Bruce and David Rocks. "How Sharp Stays on the Cutting Edge." *Business Week*, Oct. 18, 2004, 56.

5. Qualcom 2004 Annual Report, 4.

6. Foust, Dean. "Nucor: Soaring on Wings of Steel." *Business Week,* April 4, 2005, 70.

7. Caulfield (2003), 54.

8. Jayne, Vicki and Glenn Baker. "Building Critical Mass." *NZ Business*, Vol. 16 (9), 2002, 22.

Chapter Two

ECONOMIES OF SCOPE AND PRODUCT DIFFERENTIATION

Can a company prosper by offering thousands of different products? Procter & Gamble did. Founded in 1837 by William Procter and James Gamble, P&G has turned from a soap and candle producer to a consumer staples producer and distributor, selling thousands of different products to consumers, from Ivory soap to Prell, and Head and Shoulders shampoo, Tide detergent, Pampers disposable diapers, Crest dental paste, razors, coffee, pet food, etc. In 2008, the company had $83 billion in sales and $43 billion in gross profits.

P&G's success can be attributed to the mastering and executing of another well-known concept of economics, economies of scope, that supported and reinforced its leadership in consumer products, especially in the twentieth century when its labs churned scores of new consumer products. The company's stock price has soared from a few dollars in the early 1970s to $75 by 2008.

Can companies prosper by offering different versions of the same product? Sony Corporation did. Founded in the late 1940s by Akio Morita and a few other engineers, Sony Corporation churned out a number of different versions of electronic products, from the transistor in the 1950s, to the color TV in the 1960s, the VCR in the 1970s, to flat panel TVs in the early 2000s.

Sony's success can be attributed to the mastering of another economic concept, marginal product differentiation, that prolonged Sony's leadership in the consumer electronics market, especially in the 1980s when Sony was recognized as a global brand name.

What Are They?

Economies of scope are the cost savings associated with the offering for sale of different products by a single corporation rather than by different corporations. The more products offered, the higher the *total cost* savings of the products offered, and the lower the average cost per product promoted (Exhibit 2.1). This means that economies of scope arise on the demand rather than on the supply side, on the marketing, distribution, transportation, and transaction costs. Economies of scope are more evident in industries that sell a family of products that satisfy similar consumer needs, creating synergies in marketing, distribution, transportation, and transactions.

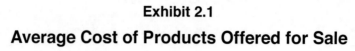

Exhibit 2.1

Average Cost of Products Offered for Sale

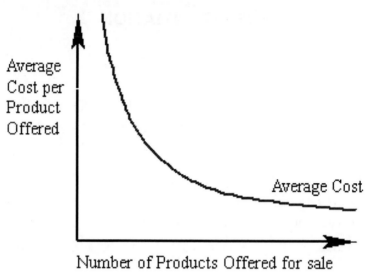

Product differentiation is the churning of different products by a corporation that cater to different market segments. The more the corporation differentiates its products, the larger the number of market segments it can address. Intel, for instance, differentiates its products by speed, media, and customization, the development of "platforms" of multiple chips catered to four market segments: home computers, computers and servers, mobile gadgets and cellular phones, and network infrastructure devices.[1] Estée Lauder's product divisions differentiate their products for different market segments. Estée Lauder targets the working woman. Clinique targets women in their twenties, while Jane targets teenagers. Applied Materials differentiates the technical characteristics of its products and services to address customers' productivity, cost, and return on investment needs. Texas Instruments customizes its analog signal products for different market segments, such as wireless, automotive, hard-disk drives, and printers. The company further customizes its digital signal processing products for several markets, including digital cameras, digital audio players, and multimedia storage disk drives. In the early 2000s, GE added more than a dozen new capabilities expected to contribute close to 90% of the company's 2005 earnings.[2]

Jack Trout argues that companies can differentiate their products in a number of ways: by identifying them with the addition of a label; by personifying them by adding consumer characters; by creating a new generic name; by changing the product name; and by repositioning the product for a new market category.[3] Rick Kash and David Calhoun argue that effective product differentiation must begin with consumer demand by identifying high profit margin consumer segments; by spotting emerging markets; by assessing areas of the market where competition is weak; by understanding the habits of the most important consumers, and so on.[4]

Product differentiation often supports and reinforces economies of scope, as different product versions enter the "sales channel." The benefits of product differentiation also accrue on the demand side, not in terms of cost savings, but in the sales gains. The demand for new products is inelastic—which allows the corporation to charge a premium over older or competing models.

Why Are They important?

Economies of scope allow companies to achieve certain synergies that lower the cost of product offerings. The pharmaceutical industry is a good case in point. The larger the number of products a pharmaceutical corporation offers, the higher the total cost savings on marketing, distribution, and transaction costs. The larger the number of products a Pfizer salesperson pitches to doctors, the lower the cost for each product marketed; the larger the order it receives from pharmacies; and the lower the transaction, distribution, and transportation costs. The consumer staples industry is another case in point. The larger the number of products P&G offers for sale, the better the company utilizes its advertising dollars, salespeople and streamlining its distribution, marketing, and transportation costs.

Product differentiation allows corporations to differentiate and distinguish themselves from the competition, expanding the number of market segments they address, while lowering the demand elasticity for the new products offered. A new iPhone, for instance, allows Apple to regain the competitive edge against imitators, while capturing the market segment of "consumer innovators," consumers who easily get bored with established products, and are willing to pay a premium over the old phone.

How Can They Be Attained?

Economies of scope and product differentiation aren't new competitive strategies. In the 1930s, automobile companies like GM differentiated their products by income, developing a broad line of automobile products catered to different market segments, for "every purpose and every purse": Cadillac for the upper class, the Oldsmobile and Buick for the middle class, and the Chevrolet for the lower class. In the 1960s and the 1970s, Japanese corporations expanded their presence in world markets by changing the attributes. Japanese automobile makers like Toyota and Honda, for instance, managed to gain substantial market share in the U.S. market by introducing smaller, more efficient, and more maneuverable cars with FWD. Japanese radio receiver makers like Sony managed to capture most of the U.S. market by miniaturizing radio receivers, while plain paper copy makers made their headway in the U.S. market by introducing simple liquid toner copiers.

Economies of scope and product differentiation can be accomplished both internally and externally. In the consumer electronics sector, Sony relies on its own resources and expertise to differentiate its products. For the period 1950–2001, Sony Corporation has successfully developed twenty-seven innovative products, including the first tape-recorder, transistor radio, VCR, "Triniton" color TV, Digital Audio Tape (DAT), and Digital Video camcorder. Nokia has also relied on its own resources to churn new products (see Exhibit 2.2). Korean conglomerates like Samsung Electronics internally produce almost every component going into their products. In the pharmaceuticals industry, Johnson and Johnson relies both on its own resources and on outside resources. The company's acquisition of McNeil Laboratories added a number of over the counter drugs popular in the U.S. market, including Tylenol. The acquisition of LifeScan, Inc. added glucose monitors, the acquisition of Neutrogena added a number of beauty aids, while the acquisition of DePuy added a number of orthopedic products. In the soft beverage industry, Coca Cola relies on its own resources for carbonated drinks, but on outside resources for non-carbonated drinks. For this purpose, the company has formed alliances and joint ventures with consumer staples companies like Nestle to provide non-carbonated drinks like iced coffee and iced tea. PepsiCo's acquisition of alternative drinks-maker South Beach Beverage Co. and Quaker Oats, owner of leading sports drink-maker Gatorade, expanded the company's drink portfolio to competing products.

In the electronic banking industry, companies rely on alliances to differentiate their products. The strategic alliance among Spain's Banco Popular, IBM, and German financial service company Allianz is a fourth case in point. The three companies agreed to create an Internet portal and to launch a business-to-business (B2B) partnership. Allianz and Banco Popular invested one billion pesetas ($5.66 million) as a seed capital for the portal. IBM provided the technology for the portal and the B2B project. In the food industry, J. M. Smuckers expanded its U.S. product portfolio by acquiring peanut-butter product maker Jif. In the networking industry, Cisco Systems and Nortel Networks relied on a stream of mergers and acquisitions. In the 1990s, Cisco acquired about seventy companies, while Nortel Networks acquired ten companies, including IP Network maker Bay Networks, Internet protocol services Shasta, and enterprise network maker Peripheronics.[5]

Exhibit 2.2

Nokia's Product Differentiation Model

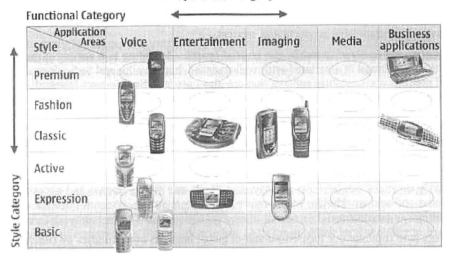

Source: Annual Reports.

Apple's Product Differentiation Matrix

Source: Inhabitat.

Each method of achieving economies of scope and product differentiation has its own advantages and disadvantages. Internal expansion allows companies to better integrate the new products into the sales channel, but they take more time to plan and implement. External expansion takes less time to plan and implement, but makes it more difficult for companies to integrate the new product into the sales channel.

Tips for Investors—Be Selective—Scope and Differentiation Doesn't Always Translate to Higher Profits and Equity Prices

The concept of economies of scope applies on the demand side. Cost efficiencies come from the synergies created by co-promoting, co-distributing, and cotransporting similar products, not from co-production—co-producing products creates diseconomies of scale. Companies that produce and offer a large number of diverse products and services experience rising costs and diminishing profitability that negatively affect equity performance. AOL-Time Warner is a case in point. The company, which is the product of the merger of three companies, Time, Warner, and AOL, has been one of the worst performers in recent years, its stock has dropped from around $80 in the early 1990s to around $8 in the early 2009.

Product differentiation often makes products too complicated for consumers to handle, especially for what marketers call the "early majority" that lacks the skills of pioneers. Product differentiation is easy to be copied and replicated by the competition. This means that it isn't sustainable over the long term.

Summary

Economies of scope are the cost savings associated with the expansion of the product line offered for sale by a corporation; the broader the product line, the higher the total cost savings—and the lower the average cost per product offered. Product differentiation is the churning of different products by the same corporation that cater to different market segments. Economies of scope are more evident in industries that provide a family of products that satisfy similar needs, creating synergies in marketing, distribution, transportation, and transaction. Product differentiation is more evident in technology industries, like consumer electronics. They allow companies to improve pricing power and to expand into new markets.

Review Questions

1. What are economies of scope?
2. What is product differentiation?

3. Which industries are most conducive to economies of scope and product differentiation?

4. How are economies of scope and product differentiation attained?

5. How do economies of scope and product differentiation contribute to a company's sustainable competitive advantage?

6. What are the limitations of this strategy?

Investment Link

Find the following information for Procter & Gamble:

> Current Stock Price
>
> Core Business
>
> Major Competitors
>
> Sales Revenue
>
> Cost of Sales
>
> Gross Profit
>
> Net Profit
>
> Profit Margin

Notes

1. Clark, Don. Change of Pace: Big Bet Behind Intel Comeback: In Chips, Speed Isn't Everything." *The Wall Street Journal*, Nov. 18, 2003, A1–A2.

2. GE 2004 Annual Report, 4.

3. Jack Trout, *Differentiate or Die: Survival in Our Era of Killer Competition*, Hoboken, NJ: John Wiley & Sons, Inc., 2008, pp. 25 and 77–79.

4. Rick Kash & David Calhoon, *How Companies Win*, New York: Harper Collins Publishers, 2010.

5. Heinzl (2000), 2.

Chapter Three

BRANDING

For years, U.S. apparel maker Nike, Inc. has delivered superior sales and profit performance, handsomely rewarding its stockholders. In the second quarter of 2008, for instance, the company's profit increased by 9% from a year earlier, reaching $391 million, while its revenue grew by 6% to $4.6 billion.

What is Nike's secret? Branding, the creation of a strong image of superior product quality among its teenage customers—a must have mentality that allows the company to charge a premium price over its competitors.

What Is It?

Branding is the creation of a superior image associated with a company and its products. Nike has a brand image in the consumer apparel industry. Coke and Pepsi have a brand image in the soft drink industry. Sony and Apple have an image in the consumer electronics industry, Intel in the semiconductor industry, McDonald's in the fast food industry, Abercrombie and Fitch in teenage apparel, and Cisco Systems in the Internet gear, etc.

A superior product image has both a rational and an emotional appeal for consumers. The rational appeal comes from objective differences between the branded product vis-à-vis its peers. The emotional appeal comes from the subjective differences between the branded product vis-à-vis its peers that often create an emotional connection of the consumer with the product.

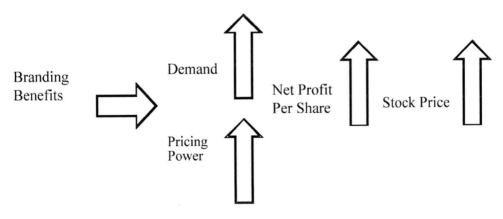

Why Is It Important?

The creation of a strong company and product image yields three types of benefits. First, it creates a strong and steady demand for the product. Second, it makes the product demand inelastic that allows the company to charge a price premium vis-à-vis its competitors. Third, branding makes it increasingly difficult for competitors to copy and imitate the product. All these factors result in higher revenues, and in higher profits over the long-term: according to a *Business Week*

Exhibit 3.1

The Value of Twenty Top Brands in 2008

Rank	Company	Brand Value* ($ millions)
1	Coca-Cola	66,667
2	IBM	59,039
3	Microsoft	59,007
4	GE	53,086
5	Nokia	35,942
6	Toyota	34,050
7	Intel	31,261
8	McDonald's	31,049
9	Disney	29,251
10	Google	25,590
11	Mercedes-Benz	25,577
12	Hewlett-Packard	23,509
13	BMW	23,298
14	Gillette	22,069
15	American Express	21,940
16	Louis Vuitton	21,602
17	Cisco	21,306
18	Marlboro	21,300
19	Citi	20,174
20	Honda	19,079

* Net present value of earnings power attributed to the company's brand
Source: Adapted from "The 100 Top Brands," *Business Week*, September 29, 2008, 56–57.

survey Coca-Cola's brand is valued at $66 billion, IBM's and Microsoft's brands at $59 billion, and GE's at $53 billion (see Exhibit 3.1). Investment in these top 100 brands in 2000 would have generated a 31% return by 2008, compared to a 28% loss of the S&P—a $100,000 portfolio consisting of these 100 brands would have grown to $131,400 over the same period.

Exhibit 3.2
Selective Brands

Product	Genuine Consumer Need Supplied
Snapple	Healthy non-carbonated drinks
Red Bull	Quick energy drinks
Barbie Dolls	Dolls for kids in a rush to grow up
iPod	Music on the go
Pokemon	Entertainment and fun for little kids
Tickle Me Elmo	Entertainment and fun for little kids
Razor Scooters	A fun sport for kids
Cell Phones	Mobile communication
PC	Office, networking
Ethernet	Networking
SUVs	"Macho" driving
Starbucks	A third place where people can share a cup of coffee and socialize with each other.
Atkins Diet	Low fat diet
Tamagotchi	A virtual pet for teenagers
Skateboards	Extreme sports
iPhone	Music, communication, networking

How Is It Attained?

Brand development requires a great deal of investment in product development, marketing, and customer relations. Successful brands begin with the consumer, with the development of a product or a service that fills genuine consumer needs and desires, a product or a service that stirs up consumer emotions. Snapple, for instance, fills the consumer need for healthy non-carbonated drinks while Red Bull fills the consumer need for energy drinks (see Exhibit 3.2). Both products stir up consumer emotions by placing them in a distinct group of cool individuals. But how can companies find out what consumers want?

By meeting, engaging, employing, and even partnering with the consumer, and by treating consumers as communities rather than as individual units, which can be accomplished in a number of ways. First, through face-to-face meetings with consumers in places that matter the most: in retail stores where they browse and test products, in the repair shop where they bring defective products for repair, in everyday life where consumers use the products, and in labs where products are designed. Sony Corporation, the electronics pioneer which has churned blockbuster products like the color TV, the VCR and the Walkman, has set up labs known as "antenna shops" inside retail stores where product engineers and designers spend their weekends talking to customers about the products they bring for repair. Samsung Electronics and LG Electronics routinely visit retail stores observing consumers browsing their products. It takes face-to-face meeting in places where consumers live and use products, as P&G management has been doing. "It is *always eye opening* to spend time with consumers to understand why they buy or do not buy P&G products. And it is always *inspiring* to understand their lives and how we can help make their everyday household and personal-care experiences more satisfying."[1]

Second, through the active engagement of customers in the product design process, where they are afforded the opportunity to define what is best for them.

Would-be authors, for instance, engage would-be readers in blogs, where readers help them shape their manuscripts' characters and plot. Japan's bestseller fiction *Train Man* is a case in point. The book began as a blog about a young man rescuing a girl from a drunk person on a train, and shaped up as a chat between the author and the members of the chat group. Some members suggested that the hero take the girl out on a date. Others suggested that he replace his glasses with contact lenses and get a stylish haircut to make himself more attractive to the girls, and so on. Another "blook," "*Demon Wife* followed the same path.[2] Companies as diverse as General Motors, Wells Fargo, Microsoft, and Intuit hire marketing consultants to track online consumer forums to improve their products.[3] Enterprise software-maker, Salesforce.com, works closely with the customer to develop enterprise solutions that cater to each customer's needs: incorporating consumer complaints and requests into upcoming software upgrades and, by monitoring software downloads, determining which features are popular and which aren't. "As Salesforce.com makes clear, their responsiveness to customer complaints and feature suggestions, you might imagine that more customers will take the time to make their own suggestions, which will further help in codesign and codevelopment."[4]

P&G's web subsidiary Reflect.com allows its beauty products customers to "voice their specific beauty needs and desires with a precision that has never been available before," that is, interact directly with beauty experts and researchers, coming up with products that cater to their specific needs. General Motor's web business unit, eGM, allows the company to connect online with dealers, and to tailor its car models to specific consumer needs. Google allows business to monitor the volume of different product queries. "Businesses are learning to use web-based services from the internet companies Yahoo, Inc. and Google, Inc. and other independent tools to evaluate the volumes of searches conducted on any given keyword. While few businesses say search data are their only source of product research or decision-making, some say it plays a useful role."[5] Popular puzzle company Nikoli that has developed Sudoku, among other things, creates forums, whereby readers can submit new puzzle ideas.[6]

By now, it has become sort of a "standard practice" for companies to receive and study feedback on line from customers. This is especially common practice in the clothes retailing industry. Customer reviews on clothes are posted on big retailer sites such as Target Corporation's Target.com, Federated Department Stores Inc.'s Macys.com, and Sears Holding Corporation's Sears.com. Big retailers from other businesses and product categories have also added customer comments to their sites. They include outdoor retailer Cabela's, Inc., Petco Animal Supplies, Inc., Home Depot ,Inc., and Bass Pro Shops. Such comments help their designers determine which models will succeed and which will fail.

Food companies, like ConAgra Foods, Inc., use the Internet to identify declining and emerging consumer trends that may affect their product portfolio. "ConAgra Foods, Inc. got an early warning from chatter on the Internet that the low-carb craze was fading. The huge food company seized the chance to promote an alternative menu, its Healthy Choice soups, entrees, and lunch meats."[7] Electronic gadget makers like Apple solicit suggestions about the "Next Big Thing," through its website AppleMatters.com. Starbucks works closely with customers to identify their tastes and preferences for different drinks.

Third, through large scale surveys, which reveal the product attributes that are most appealing to consumers. Asahi Brewery's hit, SuperDry beer, for instance, was the product of a large scale survey that revealed the product attributes the target consumer group valued the most. Hasbro's game hits are the product of online surveys of gamers as well as a close observation of children at play.

Fourth, by hiring "prosumers," i.e., consumers who work with producers to test out their products and make suggestions for new ones, rather than just consuming the end product. "In other words, customers do more than customize or personalize their ware; they can self-organize to create their own. The most advanced users, in fact, no longer wait for an invitation to turn a product into a platform for their own innovations. They just form their own prosumer communities on line, where they share product-related information, collaborate on customized products, engage in commerce, and swap tips, tools, and product hacks."[8] Toshiba, for instance, hires psychologists with music hobbies to work side by side with engineers, having them perform as potential customers to test their products. Boston-based Karmaloop asks customers to submit new product designs that are evaluated by an internal design committee. The company gives discounts to customers who provide referrals. Educational promotion video-maker Tabula Degita teams up with school administrators to develop math games.

Fifth, by partnering with consumers and sharing the risks and rewards associated with the development of new products. Office supplies retailer Staples, Inc., for instance, solicits new product ideas from consumers, whereby successful contenders receive lump-sum prizes and royalties. Netflix, a mail-order movie corporation, offers rewards to customers who will come up with ideas to improve service, while Electronic Arts pays $20,000 for the Best Short Digital animation. YouTube.com shares revenues with amateur video producers.

Sixth, by marrying art with technology. Apple's marriage of art and technology in product design has transformed the company from a computer maker into a branding machine that creates an aura over its products that turns consumer interest into passion and desire that spins out into a contagious behavior and hype that quickly reaches consumer majority. Reflecting such emotional response, iMac, for instance, has been described by consumers as "funky," "snazzy," "extremely friendly," "glowing," "accessing," "electrifying," "a revolution in the box," "an icon," while the iPhone has been described as "tantalizing," and "Jesus phone."[9]

Branding is a lengthy process that begins with the consumer, by identifying consumer needs, wants, and desires through a number of methods that reveal consumer preferences, especially methods that get the consumer engaged and involved early on, from the product design stage.

Tips for Investors—Branding May Not Survive in the Long-Term

As any other strategy, branding has three limitations. First, branding is undermined by competition, especially in the long-term, as imitators come up with similar products. Second, branding cannot help a company expand its business in saturated markets. Third, success often leads to reckless behavior that undermines the financial position of the company, as has been the case with brand name companies like

AIG, Citigroup, Countrywide Financial, Lehman Brothers, and Merrill Lynch that either collapsed or nearly collapsed in the 2008–2009 financial crisis.

Summary

Branding is the creation of a superior corporate and product image that has both rational and emotional consumer appeal. Branding fuels a strong and steady demand for the product, it strengthens pricing power, and makes it difficult for other companies to imitate and replicate the product. Brand development begins with the customer, addressing genuine needs and desires, and requires a great deal of investment in product development, marketing, and customer relations. Companies must constantly meet with customers in the places where customers buy products and engage them in product design. Branding may not survive in the long-run, as competitors come up with similar products.

Application
Nike Does It Again

Sports apparel company lights up Wall Street with strong revenue and earnings Nike Inc. has a history of beating Wall Street estimates, which it did this time around.

The footwear and athletic apparel company reported on Tuesday it earned 95¢ per share in the first quarter of 2021, almost double what analysts had anticipated. Revenue came in at $10.59 billion, ahead of the $9.11 billion expected thanks to an 82% surge in online sales.

Investors were impressed by Nike's performance, sending its shares higher in after-hours trading.

That's a vote of confidence for Nike's management, which has effectively managed capital the company's return on invested capital exceeds its weighted average cost of capital by a wide margin.

Company	ROIC %	WACC %	Excess return % (ROIC-WACC)
Nike (NKE, Financial)	15.54	5.91	6.63
Adidas AG (ADDYY, Financial)	4.25	4.07	0.23
Deckers Outdoor Corp. (DECK, Financial)	31.68	6.33	25.35

Nike accomplishes this through multiple advantages that form "moats" around its business, limiting the entry of new competitors to its market.

One of these advantages is branding, a strong image among its customer base a must-have mentality that allows the company to charge premium prices.

Then there's scale, the cost savings associated with a larger corporate size. Nike has close to $37.4 billion in revenue, almost twice its closest competitor, Adidas.

And there's scope, the cost savings associated with offering different products by a single company for sale. Nike has a broad range of shoes, clothing and gear for men, women and children.

Another advantage is innovation, the discovery of new products that have several distinct characteristics separating them from conventional competing ones these traits stir up emotions and appeal to consumers' tastes.

Nike's products have all these features, and then some. They are also known for featuring the names of professional athletes. For example, the Nike Air Jordan Retro XI sneakers are modeled after the 1996 originals designed for Michel Jordan when he played for the Chicago Bulls.

This strategy adds a sensation to Nike's products and keeps the buzz alive even when a pandemic keeps consumers confined in their homes.

Source: Gurufocus, September, 22, 2020.

Review Questions

1. What is branding?
2. How is branding attained?
3. Which industries are most conducive to branding?
4. How does branding contribute to a company's sustainable competitive advantage?
5. What are the limitations of this strategy?

Investment Link

Find the following information for Coca Cola:

Current Stock Price

Core Business

Major Competitors

Sales Revenue

Cost of Sales

Gross Profit

Net Profit

Profit Margin

Notes

1. Lafley, A. G. and Ram Charan. *The Game-Changer: How You Can Drive Revenue and Profit Growth with Innovation*. New York: Crown Business, 2008, 35.

2. Kane, Yukari I. "How *Demon Wife* Became a Media Star and Other Tales of the 'Blook' in Japan." *The Wall Street Journal*, Oct. 5, 2006. B3.

3. Kadet, Anne, "Romancing the Bloggers," *SmartMoney*, November 2006, 92–96.

4. Coburn (2006), 159.

5. Delaney, K. "The New Benefits of Web-based Queries." *The Wall Street Journal*, Feb. 6, 2007.

6. Fackler, Martin. "After Sudoku, What's Next?" *The New York Times*, March 21, 2007, C1.

7. Livingston (2006), A01.

8. Tapscott and Williams (2006), 126.

9. Fishman (1999).

Chapter Four

BUNDLING

Yum! Brands may not be a well known company on Main Street, but its product portfolio that includes well-known names such as Taco Bell, Pizza Hut, Long John Silver's, A&W, and KFC, is, especially overseas. Yum! Restaurants International operates 36,000 outlets in 110 countries, from China to Russia and Vietnam, generating close to 20% Return on Invested Capital (ROIC).

Yum! Brands secret? An effective bundling of global and local product offerings that creates unique menus for different countries.

What Is It?

Bundling is the packaging of different product characteristics to create unique consumer offerings. Chemical companies routinely raise the local content of their product offerings by adding local characteristics such as services and customer support to their global products. Dow Chemical bundles its products with a comprehensive service plan that provides its customers prompt response to any problems with its products. Automobile makers churn different bundles of standardized car features with localized car features. Honda, for instance, has developed a number of automobile models tailored to different local markets around the world.[1]

Cellular phone providers routinely bundle the global product, the cellular phone, together with local service contracts that include "anytime minutes," "night and weekend minutes," "additional minutes," "long distance minutes," and "roaming" (see Exhibit 4.1). Nokia follows other cell phone makers like Motorola and Erickson and their strategic partners bundling cell phones with local message content, karaoke music in China, video-clips in South Korea, and recorded messages in Europe. In addition, Nokia works closely with local wireless service providers to compete in local markets that are highly regulated. Software provider Autodesk has localized its products for the emerging markets of China, and most notably for Asia-Pacific and China where the company has experienced robust sales.[2]

Beverage maker Diageo mixes global drinks with local drinks and liquors to create product offerings that cater to local markets. Diageo's Gordon Edge, a mix of gin and lemon, is catered to the UK market, while Safari Luna, a mix of fruit and liquor, is catered to the Netherlands. Allied Domecq's Presidente brandy and cola mix is catered to the Mexican market, while TG, a mix of Scotch and guanana is catered to the Brazilian market. Campari's Mixx, a mix of grapefruit and Campari, is catered to the Italian and Swiss market.

Exhibit 4.1

Selected Value Propositions with Both Highly Elastic and Highly Inelastic Bundles

Value Propositions	Elastic Bundles	Inelastic Bundles
Automobiles	Engines, Brakes	Financing, Repairing, Servicing
Cellular Phones	Cellular Phone Devices	Minutes, Messaging, WAP Services
IT Business Solutions	Hardware	Software
Insurance Policies	Underwriting	Sales

Why Is It Important?

Successful bundle localization expands corporate revenues in two ways. First, through the exploitation of market niches that have been neglected as too small and too expensive to be worth the effort. Hewlett Packard, for instance, has managed to expand its presence to the Indian digital photography market by replacing the electric battery charger with a solar battery charger, and by leasing rather than selling its digital cameras to local professional photographers. Shampoo makers have also managed to expand their presence in India and other poor countries by packaging their products in small, affordable packages. Yum! Brands has managed to expand its presence in Asia and Latin America by localizing fast food menus like pizza and fried chicken—delivering superior equity performance. Second, successful localization lowers the elasticity of bundle offerings, and therefore, raises the pricing power. The more localized the bundle, the lower its price elasticity, and the higher the pricing power of the provider. Conversely, the more globalized the bundle is, the higher its elasticity, and the lower the pricing power of the provider. Exhibit 4.2 shows the relationship between the degree of localization and the pricing power of a bundle. The degree of localization is measured by the value of the bundle attributed to local characteristics, and pricing power is the inverse of the bundle price elasticity.

Exhibit 4.2

Localization Intensity and Pricing Power

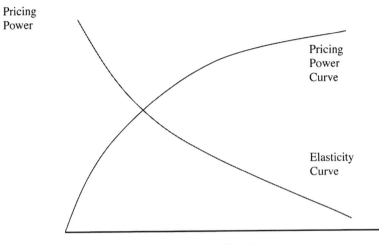

Pricing Power

Pricing Power Curve

Elasticity Curve

Degree of Localization

Source: Adapted from P. Mourdoukoutas and P. Mourdoukoutas, "Bundling in a Semiglobal Economy." *European Business Review*, Vol. 16 No. 5, 2004, p. 528.

Successful bundling results in higher revenues, and in some cases, in higher profits over the long term:

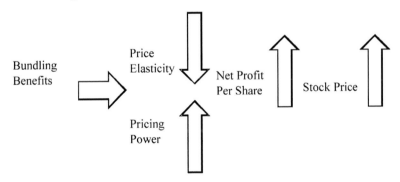

Bundling Benefits

Price Elasticity

Pricing Power

Net Profit Per Share

Stock Price

How Is It Attained?

Bundling of global and local product characteristics can be accomplished in two ways. First, internally, by setting up separate divisions to provide for both the global and the local characteristics of the bundle. Honda's factories provide the elastic components of the value proposition, the automobile, while local dealerships provide the inelastic components, sales, financing, repairing, satellite subscription, and so on. Second, externally, through strategic alliances and joint ventures. Cellular phone value propositions, for instance, are offered by alliances of cellular phone manufactures that offer the elastic component, and the cellular phone service providers that offer the inelastic component, minutes, WAP services, and billing. In some cases, alliance networks extend even among former competitors, Sandisk with Matsushita and Toshiba, Toyota with GM, Mazda with Ford, etc. (see Exhibit 4.4). Sandisk Corporation has teamed up with competitors Matsushita and Toshiba to form the Secure Digital Association or SD association for the joint development and promotion of the Secure Digital Card. The three companies will separately market and sell flash memory products developed by their joint venture FlashVision. SanDisk has further entered cross-licensing agreements with several of its competitors, including Intel, Matsushita Electric, Samsung, Sharp, and Sony. Toyota Motor Company has entered an alliance with GM to develop environmentally safe technologies, while Mazda and Ford have entered an alliance to develop fuel-cell technologies.

Tips for Investors—Bundling Has Its Own Limitations

Bundling has its own constraints and limitations. First, bundle localization becomes an easy target of imitation. Marginal localization that modifies an existing product just to keep up with the competition without adding true value to it is not sustainable. Diageo's strategy of global and local product mixes does not require symmetrical commitments by local partners and has already been matched by Allied Domecq and Campari's mixed drinks. Second, consumers are not always willing to pay premium prices for added product features. Kraft's Ooey Gooey Warm 'N Chewy Chips Ahoy!, an extension of the company's Nabisco Chips Ahoy! product portfolio is a is a case in point. Consumers found the $2.99 price too expensive and the product flopped, costing the company $5.5 million.[3] Third, by focusing on marginal product alterations companies lose sight of emerging trends in their industries. Kraft's obsession with marginal differentiation of its existing products, the Oreo and Oscar Mayer brands, contributed to the company's missing on the emerging trends in the supermarket industry.

Exhibit 4.3

Bundling of Global and Local Menus Has Delivered Superior Results for Yum! Brands

Year	Rank	Revenue ($ millions)	Profit ($ millions)
2008	253	10,416.0	909.0
2007	262	9,561.0	824.0
2006	257	9,349.0	762.0

Source: Yum! Brands Annual Reports.

Exhibit 4.4

Selective Co-Competition Agreements

Companies	Purpose of Cooperation
SanDisk, Matsushita, Toshiba	Secure digital cards
Toyota, GM	Environmental technology
Mazda, Ford	Fuel-cell technology
Honda, Isuzu, GM, Renault	Diesel engine
Renault, Nissan	Diesel engine
Toyota, BMW	Diesel engine
Ford, GM	Six step transmission

Summary

Bundling is the packaging of different product characteristics to create unique consumer offerings. Bundling is broadly used in the chemical, telecommunications, and beverage industries to raise revenues by allowing companies to exploit market niches, strengthen pricing power, and improve customer loyalty. Bundling is attained through the setting up of different corporate divisions and subsidiaries that offer complimentary goods and services, and through joint ventures and partnerships. Bundling eventually becomes the target of imitation, and often blindsides companies, missing out on emerging markets and technologies.

Application
Yum China: Right Place and Right Strategy

The company has a big plan to tap into China's fast-food market Yum China Holdings Inc. is in the right place with the right strategy to continue its winning streak on Wall Street.

The place is China's rapidly growing fast-food industry, which has helped the company reach $9 billion in sales in the last year.

The strategy is a five-year, $8 billion expansion plan, allocating more capital to high-profit new units, remodelling Kentucky Fried Chicken and Pizza Hut locations, digitizing stores, marketing and supply chain and back-office operations.

"We estimate the growth implied by this plan implies significantly more and faster growth than anticipated by investors, setting up upward revisions and valuation expansion," Quo Vadis President John Zolidis wrote in a research report published on April 15.

This week, the operator of KFC, Pizza Hut and other fast-food brands in China, reported first-quarter earnings of 54 cents per share that beat analysts' expectations of 41 cents per share.

"Our first-quarter results once again demonstrated the resilience of Yum China and were accomplished by our dedicated and tireless team of over 400,000 people," CEO Joey Wat said. "We delivered solid sales growth and operating profit amid challenging market conditions. Our operations and supply chain teams overcame a wide array of challenges and uncertainties, managed potential disruptions, and delivered robust operations for our stores."

Wall Street liked the company's results, sending its shares higher once the stock opened for trading.

Still, Zolidis thinks Yum China is a long-term buy, citing the company's growth initiatives and relative valuation.

"Over time, we see significant multiple expansions providing a basis for very attractive LT share price performance," he said. "While investors over-pay for CMG at EV 5x 2022 revenues or SBUX at EV 4x 2022 revenues, YUMC can be bought at just 2x."

Meanwhile, Yum China's recent economic profit stands at 3.22%, compared to -2.16% for Starbucks (SBUX, Financial) and -0.29% for Chipotle (CMG, Financial).

Economic profit is a measure of how effectively a company manages capital raised from stockholders and debtholders and indicates the strength of the company's competitive advantage.

Still, investors should take Zolidis' enthusiasm for Yum China with a dose of skepticism. The stock trades well above the GF Value, as are its two peers, which he uses in its relative valuation model.

Then there's the nature of the Chinese market, which isn't a homogeneous market, making further expansion a rather tricky task.

Company	ROIC	WACC	Economic Profit	Three-year Average Revenue Growth	Market Price	Intrinsic Value
YUMC	8.97%	5.75%	3.22%	1.7%	$63.15	$42.79
Starbucks	3.83%	5.99%	-2.16%	9.1%	$114.80	$77.11
Chipotle	8.50%	8.79%	-0.29%	10.4%	$1484.15	$876.15

Source: Gurufocus, April 30, 2021.

Application

Verizon: A Mature Company Still Creating Value

Some may say that Verizon Communications Inc. (VZ) is a subpar investment because it requires a ton of capital in order to remain relevent. However, in my view, this is a mature company that is still creating value for its stockholders.

It is a mature company because it is well established in its market, where it offers communications, information and entertainment products and services to consumers, businesses and governmental entities.

It creates value because it has maintained a positive economic profit over the last decade. Currently, Verizon's economic profit, as measured by the difference between return on invested capital (ROIC) and weighted average cost of capital (WACC), stands at 4.63%, which is more than three times higher than that of its peer AT&T Inc. (T):

Company	ROIC %	WACC %	ROIC-WACC % (Economic profit)
Verizon	7.96	3.33	4.63
AT&T	6.66	5.33	1.33

Verizon also beats AT&T in most critical financial performance metrics, as listed below:

Company	Verizon	AT&T
Three-year Revenue Growth (%)	0.2	-2.7
Three-year EBITDA Growth (%)	1.6	-14.2
Current Operating Margin (%)	22.45	14.65
Annual Dividend (%)	4.45	7.12
Market Price	$56.45	$29.00
Intrinsic Value	$56.07	$29.95

Economic profit is a measure of how effectively a company allocates the capital it raises in to generate profits. It is also often used as a measure of a company's competitive advantage. One of the reasons why Verizon is outperforming AT&T is because it has steered away from costly acquisitions.

Value investors also seem to have taken notice of the stock recently, including Warren Buffett (Trades, Portfolio), who added Verizon to his portfolio last week.

Like its competitors, Verizon's assets allow the company to bundle together different product offerings, a strategy that supports and reinforces its competitive edge. Bundling of Internet services with mobile services, for instance, creates customer lock-in relationships arrangements that make it costly for customers to switch to competing products.

Bundling further allows the company to achieve economies of scale, i.e. the cost benefits associated with serving a more extensive customer base with the same company assets. Average cost declines as more customers join its Internet and Mobile network.

The bottom line: Verizon is a textbook case of an oligopolistic firm that has managed to preserve economic profit, making it a more attractive value buy than competitors.

Disclosure: I own shares of Verizon Communications

Source: Gurufocus, February 23, 2012.

Review Questions

1. What is bundling?
2. How is bundling attained?

3. Which industries are most conducive to bundling?

4. How does bundling contribute to a company's sustainable competitive advantage?

5. What are the limitations of this strategy?

Investment Link

Find the following information for Yum! Brands:

Current Stock Price

Core Business

Major Competitors

Sales Revenue

Cost of Sales

Gross Profit

Net Profit

Profit Margin

Notes

1. Kotabe, M. "Efficiency vs. Effectiveness Orientation of Global Sourcing Strategy: A Comparison of U.S. and Japanese Multinational Companies." *The Academy of Management Executive* Nov. 1988, v. 12 (4), 107–121.

2. Ante, Spencer E. "Autodesk: A Software Vet's Growth Spurt." *Business Week*, April 4, 2005, 72.
   3. Ellison (2003), B1.

Chapter Five

ECONOMIES OF NETWORKING

For years, Microsoft was the "queen" of software. Its sales and profits grew by leaps and bounds, turning its founders into billionaires and many of its employees and common stockholders into multi-millionaires.

For years, eBay was the queen of online auctions. Its sales and profits soared, creating its own multi-millionaires.

What are Microsoft's and eBay's secrets? Economies of networking, the advantages associated with a product service becoming the standard for a network of users; the more users that use the product, the more valuable the product is to each user.

What Is It?

Economies of networking are the benefits associated with a larger and larger number of people using a certain product; the larger the number of people using the product, the more valuable the product to each user. The more people that use cellular phones, the more valuable cellular phones are to each consumer; the more consumers that use Microsoft Office, the more valuable the product is to each user.

Economies of networking arise on the demand side of the market, because of positive externalities, e.g., the positive effect one consumer's consumption of a product has on other consumer's consumption. The use of a cellular phone by consumer A benefits consumer B and consumer C, who are already telephone users, because there is one more person they can reach. Likewise, the use of a cellular phone by a new consumer D benefits all cellular phone users.

Economies of networking are more evident in industries conducive to network externalities, such as the information and telecommunications industries, and follow the Roger Curve of diffusion. In the beginning, a small group of consumers, called "innovators," adopt the product, followed by another small group of consumers, called "early adopters," to be followed by two larger groups, the "early and the late majority," and eventually by a smaller group called "late majority" (see Exhibit 5.1).

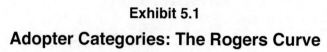

Exhibit 5.1

Adopter Categories: The Rogers Curve

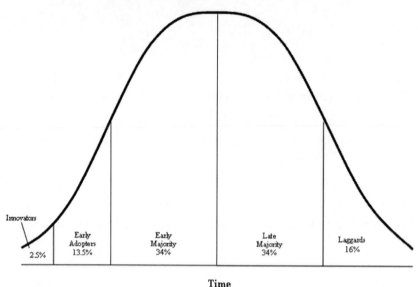

Time

Source: Adapted from Rogers, Everett M. *Diffusion of Innovation*, Third Edition. New York: The Free Press, 1983.

Why Is It Important?

Economies of networking allow companies to quickly cross the "tipping point" to reach a critical mass of consumers, which translates to soaring revenues and marketing shares, and eventually, to exponential growth in earnings and equity prices. This is especially the case in the information technology industries, whereby once the product is developed the cost of signing up an additional user or selling an additional copy of software is close to zero. Economies of networking allowed Microsoft to control 80% of the PC software, to be transformed from a small software start-up in the early 1980s to a giant by the mid-1990s, and to become one of the most successful investment stories. Economies of networking are difficult to copy and imitate. Once a product or service becomes the industry standard, it is too expensive for consumers to switch to alternative products or services.

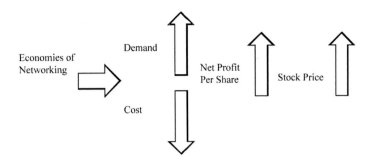

How Can They Be Attained?

The benefits of economies of networking increase exponentially once the product crosses the "tipping point," the demand level where the benefits of the product usage exceed its acquisition cost (see Exhibit 5.2).

Expected benefits and costs are both a function of the rate of the product adoption. Specifically, expected benefits, i.e., the value the product adds to consumers, are a direct function of the rate of the product adoption. Expected benefits increase exponentially with the rate of adoption, for two reasons. First, economies of networking, i.e., the more consumers adopt the product, the greater the interaction among them, and the greater the benefit to each one of them. Likewise, the more teenagers own an Xbox360, the larger the network of players, and the more valuable the game console becomes to each and every player. As more and more people, for instance, use Microsoft Word software, it becomes easier to exchange files, and therefore, the software becomes more valuable to each user. Second, the demonstration effect, i.e., the more consumers use the product, the more intimidated other consumers are to buy the product. The more children, for instance, that carry around an iPod, the more intimidated other children are to carry one around, too.

Exhibit 5.2

The Expected Costs and Benefits of Innovation Adoptions Determine the Tipping Point

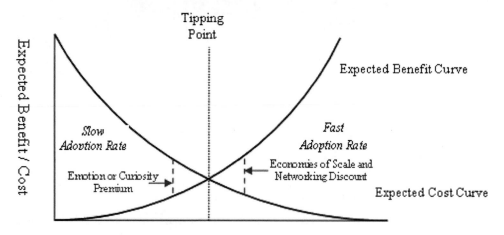

Expected costs, that is, the price the consumers pay to acquire the product, the time they spend to become familiar with it, and the perceived risk that the product fails to stand up to expectations, are an inverse function to the rate of the product adoption for two reasons. They decrease exponentially with the rate of adoption as innovators pass on the cost savings associated with a larger and larger production, while the risk of a product failing to stand up to expectations decreases.[1]

Given these patterns of expected benefits and costs, adoption rates are expected to be slow in the beginning as costs exceed expected benefits, and consumers buy the product out of emotion and curiosity rather than reason (i.e., curiosity gap); adoption rates are high when expected benefits exceed costs (known as the procrastination discount).

Reaching the tipping point requires a good knowledge of the different groups of the adoption curve, and shrewd marketing strategies to entice them into buying the product, especially the "early adopters," which are the link between the pioneers and the early majority.

Innovators. They are usually the young and restless, the better educated, venture type, the risk lovers, the most mobile and uneasy consumer group, always in discontent with their environment, always in search for something new, something different to add *excitement* to their lives. Innovators are consumer leaders, informed about new trends as featured in mass media and industry publications. They are "adventure shoppers," shopping for products that add adventure and excitement to their lives, something to show off to their peers, like the kids who started wearing old Hush Puppy Dukes and Columbias they bought in N.Y.C. thrift shops in the early 90s and fueled a subsequent sales increase of 950% by the peak of the fashion in 1996.[2]

In the IT industry, Geoffrey Moore refers to innovators as *technology enthusiasts*, people enchanted with technology per se, and determined to address their glitches, flaws, and malfunctions by collaborating with the company's technical people to troubleshoot problems. Technology enthusiasts are the "Gadget Guys."[3] Technology enthusiasts, for instance, love to show off iPhone's touch screen, and to download songs from iTunes and video from YouTube.

Innovators are the most susceptible group to mass marketing campaigns. The problem, however, is that they are usually a small group, accounting for 2.5% of the target product population (see Exhibit 5.1). They are, however, well connected to other consumer groups. Marketers must, therefore, reach this group not for its size, but for its lead purchases and in their extensive networking that makes them an important bridge to reaching the next market group, the early adopters. This is especially the case in the IT industry, where technology enthusiasts are connected with consumer bloggers and online communities, which makes them agents of influence for spreading the word about the product.

Early Adopters. Early adopters are also the young and restless, the better educated, the uneasy group of the society, always in discontent with their environment, always in search for something new to *improve* rather than to excite their lives. Early adopters are also consumer leaders, following industry and product trends; they are "ideal shoppers," shopping for new products to keep up with emerging trends.

In the IT industry, *early adopters* are *visionaries* in their market, who see technology in ways others don't, as has been the case with many legendary entrepreneurs, from Andrew Carnegie to Bill Gates. They use new technology to achieve a *revolutionary* breakthrough to gain sustainable competitive advantage in their industries. Early adopters are attracted by high-risk, high-reward projects, envisioning great gains in competitive advantage from adopting new technology. Early adopters, for instance, use the iPhone to track sales and inventories and stay in touch with customers and suppliers rather than download songs. This sort of attraction to technology makes early adopters less sensitive to the product price, provided that they can receive personalized solutions and quick response, highly qualified sales and support.

Early adopters are also an important marketing target for three reasons. First, they are a larger group than innovators, accounting for 13.5% of the target population (see Exhibit 5.1). Second, they are trendsetters. Early adopters are opinion leaders within local reference groups; they provide early insights about a product, which makes them important to identify since they influence others within their social network.[4] Third, early adopters provide the initial revenues for a new technology. Fourth, early adopters are an important group to spread the WOM to the next group, the early majority.

Early Majority. The early majority is the middle age, the less educated, the less uneasy group of society, socially active but seldom leaders. They are the deliberative decision makers, who adopt an innovation sooner than most of their social group but only after the innovation has been tested successfully with others. The early majority are the "value shoppers," looking for high quality products at reasonable prices.

Reaching to innovators and early adopters, and eventually the early majority, takes shrewd marketing strategies. In some cases, it takes exclusive agreements with product suppliers, as has been the case in the software industry. In other cases, it takes a campaign of trust, as has been the case with eBay. In a third case, it takes the active engagement of innovators in the product design, as discussed in previous chapters. In a fourth case, it takes the aggressive distribution of product samples that let consumers try to become familiar with the product. Free trials further create a sense of virtual ownership that fuels an emotional attachment of the consumer with the product. The longer consumers experience the product, the more they feel that the product belongs to them, the more likely they are to end up buying it.

Tips for Investors—Buy the Winner

In industries conducive to economies of networking, the winner takes it all, the losers get nothing. In the PC operating system, Microsoft has captured almost the entire industry. Google dominates the search engine industry, eBay dominates the online auctions industry, Amazon.com leads the online book selling industry, and Apple dominates the electronic gadget industry. Investors who have invested in these companies have been handsomely rewarded, while investors who have invested in their competitors have lost most or all of their investments.

While economies of networking protect and insulate winners from competition, from the threat of similar products, they do not protect them from other threats, like the threat from alternative products, the threat of congestion, the threat of market saturation, and the threat of government regulation. Investors must, therefore, be warned that economies of networking cannot warrant superior returns forever.

Summary

Economies of networking are the benefits associated with a larger and larger number of people using a certain product; the larger the number of people using the product, the more valuable the product to each user. Economies of networking arise on the demand side of the market and are more evident in information and telecommunications industries. Economies of networking allow companies to quickly reach a critical mass of consumers—the early majority. Attaining economies of networking requires a good knowledge of the different product adoption groups, especially the "early adopters," the link between "innovators" and the "early majority." To take advantage of economies of networking, investors must buy the winner, who takes it all.

Application

Is Groupon's Business Model Sustainable?

I am not sure whether Groupon's founders have ever read Karl Marx's and Friedrich Engels' *Communist Manifesto*. The famous little book prompts the workers of the world to unite, as they have "nothing to lose, but the chains that bind them to capitalist enterprises."

Groupon prompts consumers of the world to unite, to shop as groups rather than as individuals, so they can gain deep discounts from local businesses. But there is a catch: The discounts apply only if a certain number of customers sign up for the deal. As explained on Groupon's site: "Each day, Groupon emails its members one unbeatable offer on something great to do in your city. We offer consumers great values by guaranteeing businesses a minimum number of customers. If a certain number of people sign up, then everyone gets the Groupon offer. If that minimum isn't reached, then no one gets it."

Groupon's business model is based on a combination of "economies of networking" and "economies of scale." Typically, economies of networking are the benefits associated with a larger and larger number of consumers buying a certain product. The larger the number of people using the product, the more valuable the product to each user—as they apply to software usage. Economies of network in Groupon's model arise as soon as a threshold is reached, in the form of discounts (coupons) to consumers who participate in the network—the larger the threshold, the larger the discount. This means that economies of networking arise on the demand side of the market, as a result of the strengthening of the consumer bargaining power with product sellers.

Economies of scale are the cost savings associated with a larger production scale (size) of a certain product—the larger the production scale, the lower the per *unit* product cost. Manufacturing 1,000 laptops is cheaper than manufacturing 100 laptops. This means that economies of scale arise on the supply side of the market, on the savings from a larger production batch with the same fixed resources, on gains from improved bargaining power with suppliers.

Local businesses participating in Groupon's offerings have a dual benefit. On the one side, they can get a guaranteed demand for their products, get rid of excess capacity, and attain economies of scale. Second, and perhaps more important, Groupon's offerings create word-of-mouth buzz for new products and services, helping them reach the "tipping point."

In essence, Groupon is turning consumers into salespersons and marketers, which is nothing new. Amway and Avon (NYSE:AVP) products have been exploiting this idea for many years—though in different format, turning consumers into entrepreneurs and independent business owners, rather than spreading the word to other consumers.

While Groupon's model is simple, it isn't sustainable, for two reasons. First, as has been the case with other web-based companies like Netflix(NASDAQ:NFLX) and Open Table (NASDAQ:OPEN), Groupon is selling other companies' products who have the upper hand in any deal negotiations. Second, they have plenty of competition from direct offerings from companies and from other web-based companies with a broad user base like Google (NASDAQ:GOOG), Amazon.com (NASDAQ:AMZN), Yahoo (NASDAQ:YHOO), Expedia (NASDAQ:EXPE), Priceline.com (NYSE:PCLN), and Travelzoo (TZOO).

Compounding the problem is the product nature of Groupon deals. Most offers are in the discretionary category and services that are at the low end of the consumer list—like club memberships and cruises rather than toothpaste and laundry detergents. This means that Groupon must spend heavily on advertising to push these products and services on the top of their list, which certainly has a negative impact on the company bottom line.

The bottom line: Uniting consumers under Groupon's umbrella isn't that easy, as its business model isn't sustainable. The company has little bargaining power with product suppliers, and no barriers of entry to protect its businesses from competition.

Source: *Forbes Magazine*, October 22, 2011.

Review Questions

1. What are economies of networking?

2. How are economies of networking attained?

3. Which industries are most conducive to economies of networking?

4. How do economies of networking contribute to a company's sustainable competitive advantage?

5. What are the limitations of this strategy?

Investment Link

Find the following information for Microsoft:

> Current Stock Price
>
> Core Business
>
> Major Competitors
>
> Sales Revenue
>
> Cost of Sales
>
> Gross Profit
>
> Net Profit
>
> Profit Margin
>
> What Are Its Limitations?

Notes

1. For instance, as their production size increases, companies strengthen their bargaining power with suppliers.

2. Gladwell, Malcolm. "Annals of Style: The Cool Hunt." *The New Yorker*, March 17, 78–80.

3. Pete Blackshaw (2008), 55.

4. Rogers, Evertt M. *Diffusion of Innovations, Third Edition*. New York: The Free Press, 1983.

Chapter Six

FRANCHISING

The name McDonald's is synonymous with the word franchise, and for a good reason. It pioneered a network organization that combines the advantages of large and small organizations, economies of scale, decentralization, flexibility, and incentive compatibility between stockholders and management. Over the years, McDonald's has grown into a profitable enterprise, turning its stock into one of the most successful investments ever.

What Is It?

Franchise is a form of "collective entrepreneurship" that allows its members to share the risks and rewards associated with the discovery and exploitation of new business opportunities. The Panera Bread franchise agreement, for instance, includes a franchise fee of $35,000 per bakery-café and a royalty fee of 4–5% of sales receipts from each bakery-café. A franchise organization consists of a "core" and a collection of "peripheral units" standing at the same level, competing and cooperating with each other (Exhibit 6.1). Decision-making authority is divided between two levels, the core of the network (first level management) and the periphery at each network unit (second level management).

First level management functions as an interior and an exterior department of central government to handle common network affairs:

- Develops the vision of the organization, i.e., the rules of conduct of business among network members and between network members and third parties.

- Adopts a mission of aligning the interests of each network with those of the entire organization.

- Sets up a network communication structure that allows the sharing of information and core competencies among network members and between network members and the support office.

- Develops and brands new products.

- Negotiates joint ventures and alliances with third parties.

- Nurtures a common culture and a community of common fate and social responsibility.

Exhibit 6.1

Franchise Organizations Are Horizontal Organizations Consisting of the Core or Support Office and a Collection of Individual Franchise Units

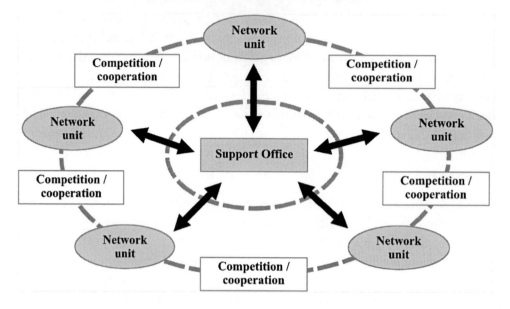

Second level management functions as a collection of local administrations handling their own internal affairs, managing their own business:

- Sets schedules, hiring of personnel, local marketing and distribution, taxation, and local community relations.

- Devises a communication structure that allows its members to interact efficiently and effectively with each other.

- Devises incentives that align the interests of each member with those of the network and the entire organization.

Why Is It Important?

A franchise organization allows network organizations to enjoy a number of distinct advantages. First, it is centralized enough to reap economies of scale—the advantages associated with a large organization that pulls together a number of services shared by its members: mentoring and networking; administrative, legal, and accounting support; marketing and advertisement. But it is also decentralized enough to reap economies of scope in personnel recruitment, local taxation, and financing. Second, the regular interaction between network units and the support office and among network units creates economies of synergy, the benefits associated with individual excellence and community dedication. A franchise organization allows network organizations to have both a global and a local presence at the same time. This creates the competitive advantages associated with a large scale of small production batches that cater products to local and regional markets. Fourth, the sharing of similar experience and the institutionalization of business networking create an entrepreneurial mind-set, and a "community of common fate." Fifth, networks can respond to changing market conditions and technologies far more rapidly than conventional hierarchical corporations. Sixth, the lowering of the business discovery cost for entrepreneurs who join the network. Seventh, each network node can become the center of a new network. This means that network organizations can grow and expand indefinitely, without the constraints and limitations of traditional hierarchical organizations (see Exhibit 6.2).

Exhibit 6.2

Business Networks Can Expand Indefinitely without the Constraints and Limitations of Traditional Organizations

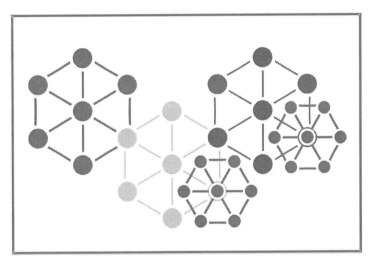

How Is It Attained?

A franchise begins with the spotting of an unfilled consumer need or an emerging consumer trend and coming up with a business concept to address it. McDonald's and Starbucks are a case in point. McDonald's is an older corporation, while Starbucks is a younger corporation. They operate in different businesses. McDonald's is in the fast food business, while Starbucks is in the coffee shop business. Yet, they both share two things in common. First, they experienced phenomenal sales growth propelled by a faddism-like consumer behaviour that reached "epidemic" proportions. Second, they both owe their success partly to the right context, the riding of emerging social trends that allowed each company to turn a market niche into a mass market.

McDonald's rode the baby-boomer trend in the 1960s, the growing ranks of teenagers and the rising participation of women in the labor force, by offering fast and inexpensive food. Their introduction of the "Speedee Service System" in 1948 established the principles of the modern fast-food restaurant. The successful expansion of McDonald's internationally transferred the American way of life to many countries around the world. Still, McDonald's needed to adapt to the social context of each country, which was accomplished by franchising to locals in many different countries.

Nowadays, McDonald's makes an effort to restore its corporate image by launching the "Simple, Bold" retail identity campaign. This is an effort to adjust McDonald's product offering to the current trends of the society. It involves the "fast" and "convenient" elements of the McDonald's concept, augmented by the "healthy" and "more natural" element which is a primary demand by consumers today. Although McDonald's primarily sells hamburgers, french-fries and soft drinks, it has added salads, fruits, and carrot sticks to its menu. Photographer Leigh Beisch photographed real ingredients in natural light in order to convey McDonald's commitment to "fresh tastes." The objective of the store was to have consumers entering a McDonald's restaurant feel that they enter the brand itself. The menu items are shown in a much more natural state compared to the artistically crafted food items that dominated before. The objective was to achieve a branded, updated and more natural look and feel at the restaurants.

Starbucks also rode the baby boomer trend in the 1990s and the Internet revolution that fuelled the need for public places to fill in the gap of the missing interaction. "Other trends of the 1990s also nourish the growth of such gathering places. More and more people are working from home offices, telecommuting by phone and fax and modem with distant offices. They go to coffee shops for the human interaction they need on regular basis."

Starbucks offered baby-boomers and ailing telecommuters a "third place," an "affordable luxury," where they could share and enjoy a cup of coffee with friends and colleagues, away from work and home. Despite the addictive, almost epidemic, qualities of coffee, Starbucks does not owe its "epidemic" growth to the magic bean. The chain has inserted itself into the American urban landscape more quickly and craftily than any retail company in history—and has forever changed the way Western companies market themselves to consumers. Sure, Starbucks is no

McDonald's—which serves 50 million customers a day at its 30,000 restaurants—but it has come close to it.

Starbucks would not have worked twenty years ago (The Right Place and Time). People weren't drinking coffee and the demographics weren't just right. Starbucks offered an antidote to an overworked culture, somewhere to just hang out. It eased the problem of social disconnection, while offering an item that made people feel coddled and tranquil. It became America's version of the British pub (Adjustment of the Message to the Context). Starbucks filled America's need for a public gathering spot—what sociology Professor Ray Oldenburg called a "third place," with home and work being places one and two. This became Starbucks' community rallying cry: It wasn't a coffee company, but a place for bringing people together through the social glue of coffee (The Right Social Context).

The secret behind Starbucks magnetic pull lies in the extraordinary amount of control it exercises over its image. At Starbucks, nothing is accidental. Everything the customer interacts with, from the obsessively monitored store environment down to the white paper cups, is the product of deliberation and psychological research. The coffeehouse as we know it is a calculated creation, tweaked and refined in large part by Howard Schultz—Starbucks' charismatic, Brooklyn-born chairman—and his army of designers. In an age when homogenous ad campaigns cover every surface that can be bought, Starbucks chose a novel marketing approach: It became an ad for itself. Stores became billboards, cups and bags mobile brand beacons. No longer would consumers just grab coffee; they would reach for the "Starbucks Experience."

Tips for Investors—Buy the Winner, but Watch for Challengers

Investing in a franchise company can be very rewarding, especially if investment takes place early on, as the franchiser experiences exponential growth. But it can be very risky, especially if the investment takes place later on, as the franchiser experiences a slow or even declining growth rate. Starbucks is a case in point. Investors who invested in the company in the mid-1990s, as it opened one store after another in prime locations, saw their investment soar. By contrast, investors who jumped in the bandwagon in early 2000, as store-opening expanded into nonprime locations, saw their investment plummet. Investors must further learn to distinguish between franchises that ride on an ephemeral fashion and faddism trend, and franchises that ride on a secular trend.

Summary

A franchise is a bottom up organization, a form of collective entrepreneurship that allows its members to share the risks and rewards associated with the discovery and exploitation of new business opportunities. It consists of a "core" and a collection of "peripheral units" standing at the same level, competing and cooperating with each other. A franchise organization allows network organizations to enjoy a number of distinct advantages. First, it is centralized enough to reap the benefits of economies of scale—the advantages associated with a large organization that pulls together a number of services shared by its members: business mentoring and networking; administrative, legal, and accounting support; marketing and advertisement. Investing in franchise companies can be very rewarding for investors, especially in the early stages as the franchise expands in prime locations.

Application

McDonald's Winning Strategy, at Home and Abroad

Of all established companies that have managed to endure the many challenges time brings their way, one stands out: McDonald's. On Friday morning, the company reported another blockbuster quarter on both the bottom and top lines, with sales rising across all geographic regions. How does the company do it?

Two ways: First, with a franchise business model that allows its franchisee-members, management, and shareholders to share the risks and rewards from the discovery and exploitation of new business opportunities—McDonald's model has become the norm for other franchise organizations. Second, by adaptation and innovation, coming up with fresh products and services to address the needs of a diverse consumer market—as shaped by demographic, economic, and local factors around the world.

McDonald's rode the baby-boomer trend in the 1960s, the swelling ranks of teenagers and the rising female labor force participation, supplying a fast and inexpensive menu. In the 1970s and the 1980s, the company rode the globalization trend by transferring the American way of life to many countries around the world. At the same time, it adapted to the social context of each county by franchising to local entrepreneurs.

In the 1990s and early 2000s, McDonald's made successful efforts to restore its corporate image by launching the "Fast and Convenient" campaign that involved the radical adjustment of the company's product portfolio to emerging food industry trends—the refurbishment of McDonald's restaurants to achieve a banded, updated, and more natural dining environment. The "fast" and "convenient" elements of the McDonald's concept were augmented by the "healthy" and "more natural" element, by adding salads, fruits, and carrot sticks to the menu.

In recent years, McDonald's has continued to broaden its product portfolio by offering high quality coffee and healthy drinks (either through its traditional restaurants or the Cafés), competing head to head with Starbucks and local cafeterias—benefiting from local trends like austerity in Europe, and robust growth in China.

Source: *Forbes Magazine*, April 20, 2012.

Review Questions

1. What is a franchise?
2. How is a franchise attained?
3. Which industries are most conducive to franchising?
4. How does franchising contribute to a company's sustainable competitive advantage?
5. What are the limitations of this strategy?

Investment Link

Find the following information for McDonald's:

Current Stock Price

Core Business

Major Competitors

Sales Revenue

Cost of Sales

Gross Profit

Net Profit

Profit Margin

What Are Its Limitations?

Note

1. Schultz and Yang (1997), 121.

Chapter Seven

INNOVATION

An iPod isn't the only product that lets people enjoy music on the go. So does a walkman player. Yet, the iPod is an innovative product that has a number of distinct and separate advantages over a traditional walkman. It is a pocket size slick machine, the match of engineering craftsmanship and art design that can upload scores of songs rather than the songs of a single CD; and it is consistent with an emerging trend, people loaded with sleek high-tech gadgets that let them listen music on the go.

LCD TV sets are more expensive than traditional tube TV sets. But they are an innovative product that has a number of advantages over tube TV sets. LCD TV sets are elegantly designed; they take less space in the living room and can be mounted on the wall like art; and they are "cool" and "hot," they make people feel different, they make them stand out from the crowd.

Teenagers love computer games. They love the characters and the action; they love a large and high resolution screen; and they love to be masters of the hot new games. Microsoft's Xbox360 game console offers all that and much more: the ability to play online against their friends. The Xbox is further consistent with an emerging trend whereby cyberspace has substituted the neighborhood as a playground for *teenagers*.

From McIntosh, to iMac, to iPod and the iPhone, Apple is certainly second to none in electronic gadgets. How does Apple do it?

Through innovation that extends to every aspect of the product supply chain, from design and branding to manufacturing and sales. For some of its products, Apple combines art and technology to outsmart the competition. iPods and iPhones marry art with technology, having a number of distinct advantages over their close competitors, Zune and BlackBerry, respectively.

What Is It?

Innovation is the discovery and exploitation of new products, new processes, and new business models. Innovative products have a number of distinct and separate features from those of conventional competing products that stir up emotion and desire, seducing consumer fantasy. Snapple, for instance, is a naturally brewed tea with healthy ingredients that serves the needs of consumers better than conventional carbonated products, while Red Bull is an Asia-based energy drink adapted to Western tastes of energetic individuals. On the other hand, the digital audio tape (DAT) had neither advantage compared to CDs and DVDs and, as a result, never took off. The same is true for Motorola's ROKR phone that tried to marry cellular phones with iPods. The devise was chunky and poorly designed, had no distinct advantages over competing models, and therefore, failed to stir consumer interest and desire.

Innovative products are further consistent with emerging lifestyles that give them a spin of "coolness." Snapple is further consistent with the emerging trend for healthy non-carbonated products, while Red Bull is consistent with the emerging trend for energy drinks. Barbie dolls were designed to look like adults rather than infants. Coolness makes innovative products fun to own. "Today the word (cool) means not only 'excellent' but also suggests an element of being "fun" and even possessing a particular attitude even in the case of inanimate objects (such as products). For example, many people consider Apple's iPod to be cool. The Volkswagen Beetle is cool. Snowboarding, the Web, Linux, Pokémon cards—all are considered cool, in some way."[1] The same is true for Nike, Adidas, and Heely's footwear. Many people find Starbucks a cool place, a "taste of romance," an "affordable luxury," an "oasis," and a "place for casual interaction."[2]

iPods and iPhones marry art with technology, having a number of distinct advantages over their close competitors, Zune and BlackBerry, respectively. The iPod has a bigger screen than Zune that is friendly to the users' eyes; it's wheel rather than button operated; and provides access to a larger library of songs (see Exhibit 7.1). The iPhone has a larger screen than BlackBerry, a better (virtual) keyboard, a GPS map, and a unique configuration of internet, phone, iPod, and a calendar tool (see Exhibit 7.2).

Exhibit 7.1

Selected Advantages of iPod over Zune

Product	Screen Size	Song Access	Song Library
iPod	2 inches	touch sensitive click driven	large Apple iTunes store
Zune	2.5 inches	click driven	small Microsoft store

Exhibit 7.2

Selected Advantages of iPhone over BlackBerry

Product	Screen Size	Music Capabilities	Keyboard	GPS Map
iPhone	large 3.5 inches, touch sensitive	4 or 8 gigabytes	virtual touch sensitive	yes
BlackBerry	small, not touch sensitive	none	physical button operated	yes

Innovative products stir up intense controversy in the mass media or cyberspace, increasing consumer awareness, creating an aura over the product that charges consumer emotions, turning interest into burning desire, seducing the consumer mind. Snapple tea is a good case in point. The company bottled the product in distinct glass containers that displayed a "circle K" on the label (indicating that the product is kosher-certified). In the early 1990s, not everyone thought so, however, as rumors spread that the K on the Snapple bottle was some kind of endorsement from Ku Klux Klan and Operation Rescue, drew a great deal of public controversy. The appointment of Wendy Kaufman as a spokeswoman (the Snapple Lady) and an endorsement from Howard Stern dashed these rumors, while creating an aura over the product. Sales caught fire, turning the product into a cascade. The announcement of the iPhone stirred controversy over its name with Cisco Systems, claiming that it has used the name first.

Why Is It Important?

Innovation is a form of entrepreneurship, the "other function" of every business enterprise, and the ultimate source of competitive advantage, especially in the highly competitive markets. In contrast to other functions of a business enterprise, entrepreneurship cannot be performed simply by hiring entrepreneurs, but is nurtured within two sets of institutions that release the individual and collective ingenuity and creativity of corporations. Innovation benefits companies in several ways. First, it allows companies to overcome competition from imitators. Intel's stream of new chips, for instance, allows the company to stay ahead of other semiconductor companies that are anxious to invade its turf. Second, it allows companies to overcome competition from alternative products. Third, it allows companies to overcome market saturation. Corning's development of flat glass, for instance, the primary material for flat panel TVs, helped the company overcome the saturation in the traditional CRT TV.

Innovative companies enjoy superior profit margins, and equity returns. For the period 1995–2005, for instance, Apple enjoyed an average annual margin growth of 7.1%, and an average equity return of 24.6%, while 3M enjoyed a 3.4% margin growth and a 11.2% equity growth (see Exhibit 7.3).

Exhibit 7.3

The *Business Week* Top Twenty-Five Innovative Firms in 2008

	Margin Growth (1995–2005) (%)	Stock Returns (1995–2005) (%)
1. Apple	7.1	24.6
2. Google	NA	NA
3. 3M	3.4	11.2
4. Toyota	10.7	11.8
5. Microsoft	2	18.5
6. General Electric	5.7	13.4
7. Procter & Gamble	4.4	12.6
8. Nokia	0	34.6
9. Starbucks	2.2	27.6
10. IBM	-0.7	14.4
11. Virgin	NA	NA
12. Samsung	-4.5	22.7
13. Sony	-11	5.1
14. Dell	2	39.4
15. IDEO	NA	NA
16. BMW	9.1	14.2
17. Intel	-0.3	13.8
18. eBay	13.0	NA
19. IKEA	NA	NA
20. Walmart	1.9	16.2
21. Amazon	25.0	NA
22. Target	7.4	25.2
23. Honda	8	12.9
24. Research in Motion	57.0	NA
25. Southwest	-0.1	13.9

Source: http://www.businessweek.com/magazine/content/06_17/b3981413.htm.

How Is It Attained?

Successful innovations add value to consumers vis-à-vis traditional products; they are consistent with emerging trends and beliefs; and they stir controversy that often turns them into cultural status symbols, attracting the interest of a critical mass of consumers. Some are innovative products that are developed by accident, while others are a result of a prolonged experimentation, and still others are developed by matching technology and art. Their adoption rate depends on the expected benefits and costs. In the beginning, as expected costs exceed expected benefits, adoption rates are low. Eventually, expected benefits exceed expected costs, and adoption rates accelerate. Product attributes, such as simplicity and ease of use, can speed up the rate of adoption, provided that they target the right consumer group. But how do innovations come about? What does it take?

First, product innovations come in a flash of light, just from a simple observation of something new, something different. The creation of Barbie dolls, for instance, came as Mattel co-founder Ruth Handler observed her daughter and her friends express a preference of playing with adult-like, rather than baby-like, dolls. The creation of Red Bull came as its creator, Dietrich Mateschitz, observed how Thai beverage Krating Daeng gave energy to air travelers.

Second, innovations emerge after a prolonged period of experimentation with different product ideas. It took Snapple creators Leonard Marsh, Hyman Golden, and Arnold Greenberg, for instance, fifteen years of experimentation with different types of apple sodas and seltzer water before they came up with Snapple tea. It took Pepsi and its Japanese partner Suntory two years of experimentation with different fruits and vegetable juices to develop a Cucumber Soda for the Japanese market.

Third, innovations are the product of "different thinking" that brings together art and technology. Apple's iPod, for instance, is the product of pioneering engineering and elegant design, as is the case with Motorola's RAZR cell phone.

Fourth, innovations could also be the product of collective efforts of different corporate departments and divisions, involving scores of engineers and marketers scattered within and without the boundaries of large corporations, out of love for ideas and the personal and professional fulfillment that comes with success. "New ideas can come from anywhere. So many ideas come not from the individual inventor tinkering away in his garage, or even in the large corporate research laboratory, but from the collective efforts of groups of people. We see these groups of idea creators motivated by their love of the idea itself and by their devotion to a process of working with nothing more than the great feeling that comes with success."[3] Microsoft Windows, for instance, is the product of scores of teams of engineers and marketers contributing the different pieces of knowledge that pulled the product together and turned it into a huge success. Motorola's and Plantronics Bluetooth headsets are the product of cooperation between the two companies' engineers and fashion designers from consumer product designers like Oakley and Dolce & Gabbana. Hasbro's electronic game hits are the result of a global network of inventors.

Fifth, innovations come by matching core corporate capabilities with emerging market opportunities. Corning's multi-billion fiber optic cable and LCD are two good cases in point. The company matched its core capabilities of glass processing with the rise of the Internet in the first case and the need for smaller, elegant computer and TV screens in the later case. In another case, it takes the "striking of a new path," to quote J. D. Rockefeller, i.e., do something unconventional, like selling computers directly to consumers, as did Dell Computer, or selling books on line as Amazon.com did.

Sixth, innovations come through acquisitions. Hasbro's acquisition of the Tonka Corporation in 1991, for example, allowed the company to expand its product portfolio to include Tonka, Play-Doh, Easy-Bake Oven, Nerf, Monopoly, and a broad range of licensed properties such as *Batman* and *Star Wars*. Cisco Systems' strategic acquisitions allowed the company to expand its product portfolio. PepsiCo's acquisition of alternative drinks maker South Beach Beverage Company and Quaker Oats, owner of leading sports drink maker Gatorade, expanded the company's drink portfolio to competing products. Strategic acquisitions are the acquisitions of smaller corporations, often start-ups, by larger corporations paid for by cash or equity that nurture entrepreneurship in a number of ways. First, strategic acquisitions allow large corporations to accelerate their entry to emerging markets that often undermine their core business, i.e., to overcome the "innovator dilemma." Cisco Systems strategic acquisitions allowed the company to expand its portfolio of products, achieving economies of scale and scope at the same time. Novellus Systems acquisition of GaSonics International Corporation allowed them to expand thier presence to the wafer surface preparation business, while the acquisition of German lapping and polishing equipment maker Peter Wolters allowed the company to expand beyond semiconductor manufacturing. Coca-Cola's acquisition of Russian juice-maker Multon Co. allowed the company to expand its presence into the country's emerging market for soft drinks. Telefonica's acquisition of a 51% stake in Cesky Telecom gave the Spanish telecommunications company access to the Czech Republic market.

Tips for Investors—Innovation Is an Expensive and Risky Strategy

Innovation requires the amassing of a great deal of resources and talent. Innovative companies must constantly plow a large part of their sales receipts to R&D, which leaves little room for policies that enhance stockholder value, such as dividend and share buy-back. Innovations further follow an irregular pattern that makes sales and earnings growth erratic and unpredictable. For every Intel, there is Advanced Micro Device, and for every Apple, there is Motorola. That's why legendary investors like Warren Buffett steer away from technology stocks.

Summary

Innovation is the discovery and exploitation of new products, new processes, and new business models that add value to the consumer. Innovation is a form of entrepreneurship, the "other function" of every business enterprise, and the ultimate source of competitive advantage, especially in the highly competitive markets. In contrast to other functions of a business enterprise, entrepreneurship cannot be performed simply by hiring entrepreneurs, but must be nurtured within two sets of institutions that release the individual and collective ingenuity and creativity of the members of corporations. Innovation is pursued with institutions and policies that lower the internal and external boundaries of traditional corporations. Innovation is an expensive and risky strategy—that's why some legendary investors steer away from technology companies.

Application

Google's Two Secrets of Success

For the July–September quarter, Google earned $2.7 billion or $8.33 per share, a 26% increase over $2.2 billion or $6.72 per share from a year ago—easily beating the most optimistic analysts' estimates. Revenues increased 33% to $9.72 billion.

Google's startling performance raises anew the question: What is Google's success secret? How can a company amass $9.7 billion in revenue, mostly from advertising?

The answer to the first question is certainly leadership and innovation in the fastest growing areas of search engines, multimedia, and smartphones. As with other successful technology companies like Apple, Oracle Corporation (NASDAQ:ORCL), and Salesforce.com (NYSE:CRM), Google is a customer-centered company—its innovation process begins and ends with the customer.

The answer to the second question is collective entrepreneurship—Google's other secret to success.

Collective entrepreneurship is a network organization that allows a diverse group of people to share the risks and the rewards associated with the discovery and exploitation of new business opportunities. Google's Blogger service, for instance, allows bloggers to set up their own blogs promoting ideas and products; viewers to get access to these products and ideas; and advertisers to pitch their own products and services to viewers.

In other words, Google is in a collective entrepreneurship with bloggers, advertisers, and viewers sharing the risks and rewards from the discovery and exploitation of new business opportunities—a stroke of genius by company founders. Successful blocks that attract a great deal of traffic reward all parties: viewers get the information or the product they search for; advertisers make their products and service available to the right audience; and bloggers and Google share the advertising revenues. By contrast, unsuccessful blogs that fail to attract traffic result in losses to all parties. Viewers waste their time, as they don't find what they need; advertisers have no audience for their commercials; and bloggers and Google have no revenues to share—Google wastes their cyberspace, and bloggers waste their time to post whatever material they post.

The bottom line: Google isn't just a technology innovator. It is a business model innovator.

Source: *Forbes Magazine*, October, 13, 2011.

Application
IBM's Hopes Are in the Cloud

January 25, 2021

IBM's (IBM) hopes for a revenue rebound in 2021, which is intrinsically tied to its hybrid cloud and AI, according to a statement by its chairman Arvind Krishna:

"We made progress in 2020, growing our hybrid cloud platform as the foundation for our clients' digital transformations while dealing with the broader uncertainty of the macro environment. The actions we are taking to focus on hybrid cloud and AI will take hold, giving us the confidence we can achieve revenue growth in 2021."

Krishna's statement followed Big Blue's 2020 fourth-quarter and full-year results, which showed a 4.6% revenue decline in 2020, underlining its chronic revenue decline problem and lackluster Wall Street performance.

The IT giant's shares have been heading south since 2013, ranking at the bottom of Dow Jones components. Apparently, investors have been looking for better opportunities in the IT sector, to companies with positive economic profit.

Economic profit, calculated as return on invested capital (ROIC) minus weighted average cost of capital (WACC) is a measure of how effectively a company manages capital to deliver superior returns to its holders and an indicator of the strength of the company's competitive advantage. A negative economic profit means that the company destroys value as it grows and that its competitive advantage is eroding by competition or market saturation.

Company	ROIC %	WACC %	Economic Profit % (ROIC-WACC)
Amazon	11.37	7.97	3.41
Microsoft	28.10	5.89	22.21
Google	20.93	7.26	13.67
IBM	5.64	5.82	-0.18

Source: Compiled from Gurufocus, January 23, 2021.

To turn revenues around, IBM's previous and current leadership have launched a radical restructuring of the company, shedding mature, slow-growing technology businesses and replacing them with emerging high-growth areas like the "hybrid" multi-cloud market. That's a computing environment that combines multiple cloud providers and clouds, a $91.74 billion industry according to Statista.

IBM's strategy is based on the premise that corporate clients view the cloud opportunity as incorporating their on-premises facilities, private clouds and public clouds.

To speed up corporate restructuring, the technology giant paid big bucks to acquire Red Hat a couple of years ago. The open-source technology company provided IBM with an innovative hybrid cloud platform and a vast open-source developer community.

Still, corporate restructurings are a slow and painful process. Usually, things turn worse before they get better, as the new businesses do not grow fast enough to make it up for the lost revenue and profits in the old businesses. While IBM has made good progress in its foray into the cloud business, it lags behind the early movers and the giants like Amazon (AMZN), Microsoft (MSFT) and Alphabet's Google (GOOG)(GOOGL).

The Covid-19 pandemic has compounded IBM's restructuring problems by hurting its legacy business, as corporate clients cut down spending on hardware and operations.

Big Blue reported fourth-quarter revenues from its Systems (includes Systems Hardware and Operating Systems Software) segment of $2.5 billion, down 17.8% (19.4% adjusting for currency) from a year earlier due to declines in all Systems Hardware platforms.

While it's still unclear whether IBM's bet on cloud and AI will pay off, one thing is clear: Wall Street is looking elsewhere in the IT space for profitable opportunities.

Application

Intel: A New CEO and Old Problems

Intel Corp. (INTC) has a new CEO but old problems: technology missteps, falling market share, lackluster performance on Wall Street and hedge fund activism.

Last week, the chipmaker took a radical step in addressing these problems, appointing Pat Gelsinger, an Intel alumnus, as its new CEO after Bob Swan stepped down.

Wall Street cheered the move. Intel stock closed up 4% at $59.25 on Thursday after advancing 7% on Wednesday, following the CEO change announcement. BMO Capital Markets raised its target for the stock to $70 from $50 early Thursday.

Still, Intel's Wall Street performance has lagged far behind competing chipmakers like Advanced Micro Devices (AMD) and Nvidia (NVDA). The company's shares are up 17% over the last 24-month period, while AMD's shares have gained 337% and Nvidia's shares rose 236%.

Intel also lags behind AMD and Nvidia in a couple of common financial and economic metrics, including average annual total return over the last decade and economic profit, a measure of how effectively a company manages shareholder and debtholder capital.

Company	INTC	AMD	NVDA
Three-year Revenue Growth (%)	9.7	5.1	18.4
Three-year EBITDA Growth (%)	21.5	–	18.5
Current Operating Margin (%)	31.81	13.27	27.17
Average Annual Total Return (2010–2020)	13.97	26.97	37.57
Market Price	$57.58	$88.21	$514.38
GF Intrinsic Value	$61.57	$40.32	$373.47
Economic Profit (ROIC-WACC)%	14.89	25.40	37%

Meanwhile, Intel lags behind Taiwan Semiconductor Manufacturing (TSM) in the chip manufacturing process, still struggling to make chips at 7 nanometers when Taiwan Semiconductor is already manufacturing chips at 5 nanometers. And one of its big customers, Apple (AAPL), no longer uses its processors in Mac computers.

Intel's leadership change comes amid a turnaround in its traditional business segment and in the emerging cloud-computing segment, which has experienced substantial growth in recent years.

But these efforts weren't sufficient to appease hedge fund activists like Third Point Management's Daniel Loeb (Trades, Portfolio), who called for the company to explore strategic alternatives to enhance shareholder value.

Still, fixing Intel's woes won't be easy for the new leadership team either, which will have to make a hard decision: Choose between sticking with its long tradition of integrating design and manufacturing and keeping them internally (insourcing) or outsource manufacturing as its competitors AMD and Nvidia have been doing.

Insourcing versus outsourcing of manufacturing is an old dilemma many American technology companies have been facing, as they are advantages and disadvantages to each choice. Insourcing helps companies better protect their technological breakthroughs, but it can slow things down while raising costs, giving competitors an edge.

Outsourcing, on the other hand, improves efficiency, cuts costs, speeds up product development and allows companies to focus on their "core competencies." But has its own limitations and "unintended consequences" that, if not addressed, can turn it into a bad business strategy.

Outsourcing is easy to be replicated by the competition; it leads to fragmentation and disintegration of the supply chain, inviting new competitors into the industry. It also nurtures corporate complacency and undermines a company's relations with its labor, customers and the domestic and local communities. Hewlett-Packard (HPE) and IBM (IBM) are among the American companies that know too well the unintended consequences of outsourcing.

While it's unclear which way Intel's new leadership will go, one thing is clear: They have a tough road ahead.

Source: Gurufocus, January 18, 2021.

Review Questions

1. What is innovation?

2. Why is it important?

3. How is innovation attained?

4. What is the relationship between innovation and entrepreneurship?

5. Why do legendary investors stay away from technology stocks?

Investment Link

Find the following information for Apple:

> Current Stock Price
>
> Core Business
>
> Major Competitors
>
> Sales Revenue
>
> Cost of Sale
>
> Gross Profit
>
> Net Profit
>
> Profit Margin

Notes

1. Gloor and Cooper (2007), 7.
2. Schultz and Yang (1997), 119.
3. Gloor and Cooper (2007), 2.

Chapter Eight

MARKET POWER

For years, Moody's and S&P, the two credit grade agencies survived and thrived, rewarding their stockholders handsomely. Their secret?

Market power. Moody's and S&P is a duopoly, a market with two competitors. Market power provides Moody's and S&P pricing power, the ability to raise price without losing a substantial share of their business. Over time, higher price results in higher revenues and higher profits, the primary driver of higher stock prices.

Moody's and S&P aren't the only companies that enjoy market power. Utility and cable companies, companies, like Duke Energy, Southern Company, and American Electric Power, and Cablevision have also market power, as they are local monopolies. The same is true for pharmaceutical companies like Amgen that are the sole providers of vital drugs.

Market power arises from market control, the ability of a firm or a group of firms to deter or even block entry of new competitors to the industry, as is discussed in further detail in the remainder of this chapter.

What Is It?

Market power comes in two forms: industry market power and individual firm market power. Industry market power is the ability of an entire industry to raise prices without losing a substantial portion of its customers. Individual firm power is the ability of one firm to raise its prices without losing a substantial portion of its customers to other firms within the industry.

Industry market power is most evident in non-discretionary consumer industries, such as food and beverage, tobacco, property insurance, and pharmaceuticals (see Exhibit 8.1). Conversely, industry market power is less evident in industries producing discretionary items, such as furniture, appliances, and automobiles. Individual firm market power is more evident in industries conducive to one of the factors discussed in the previous chapters, economists of scale and scope, economies of networking, etc., and in industries where firms can hold special rights to a specific product or service.

Exhibit 8.1

Market Power for Selective Industries

Industry	Market Power
Food and Beverage	High
Property Insurance	High
Pharmaceuticals	High
Tobacco	High
Furniture	Low
Toys	Low
Entertainment	Low
Clothing	Low

Why Is It Important?

High industry market power lowers the elasticity for the industry's products, allowing the firms in the industry to raise prices without losing a substantial portion of their customers. High market power, for instance, makes demand for food and beverage and pharmaceuticals inelastic, and therefore, allows companies in these industries to raise prices (see Exhibit 8.2). Low industry market power raises the elasticity for the industry's products, preventing the firms in the industry from raising their prices. Low market power, for instance, makes demand for furniture, toys, and entertainment elastic, limiting the pricing power of firms in these industries to raise prices.

Market power is particularly important in times the economy is faced with cost shocks like rising prices for raw and energy materials that raise production and transportation costs across the economy. Industries with high pricing are in a better position to pass on these costs to consumers, maintaining profitability, while industries with low pricing power must absorb part or all of these costs, seeing their profitability eroding.

Industry market power can be supported and reinforced by firm-specific market power. Strong brand name companies, for instance, have more power to raise prices than generic name companies. Likewise, leaders in innovation have more power to raise prices than laggards, as discussed in the previous chapters.

Exhibit 8.2

Market Power for Selective Industries

Industry	Market Power	Elasticity	Pricing Power
Food and Beverage	High	Low	High
Property Insurance	High	Low	High
Pharmaceuticals	High	Low	High
Tobacco	High	Low	High
Furniture	Low	High	Low
Toys	Low	High	Low
Entertainment	Low	High	Low

How Is It Attained?

Industry market power is attained in two ways. First, by limiting the number of substitute products by launching legislation campaigns that make industry products mandatory. Second, by changing the nature of the product in relation to income, by launching successful marketing campaigns that turn industry products from nondiscretionary to discretionary.

Individual market power can be attained in one of the ways we discussed in the previous chapters, through economies of scale and scope, branding and bundling, and product differentiation and innovation, and through industry consolidation, that is, the limiting of the number of competitors.

Tips for Investors—Market Power Doesn't Last Forever

Market power doesn't last forever. Every industry and company is faced with three threats: First, imitation from similar products. Another industry, another firm comes up with a similar product intensifying competition and undermining pricing power. Second, competition from alternative products. Another industry, another firm comes up with radically different products that undermines the very existence of the industry. Third, market saturation. Every industry has a maximum number of consumers to be served. As the industry approaches this maximum, market pricing fades away.

Application

Air Products' Selloff Is a Buying Opportunity

Air Products and Chemicals Inc.'s (APD) recent selloff is a buying opportunity for long-term investors.

Shares of the atmospheric and specialty gases giant lost close to 10% of their value on Wednesday following a disappointing fourth-quarter earnings report. The selloff continued into Thursday with Air Products shares losing another 6% by mid-day.

Air Products reported GAAP earnings of $2.19 per share, trailing analysts' consensus estimate of $2.21. Revenue came in at $2.32 billion, exceeding expectations of $2.26 billion.

Apparently, investors expected more from Air Products to justify the big run-up of its stock ahead of the earnings report.

But it could also be argued that the selloff is unjustified for several reasons.

First, the company's results have been negatively affected by the Covid-19 crisis, which reduced demand from its industrial customers like oil refiners. Management estimates that headwinds from the pandemic shaved 15 cents to 20 cents off its earnings.

Then there's the nature of the company's products, which are used by hospitals, semiconductor manufacturers and refineries, with little competition.

That makes them price inelastic, allowing Air Products to raise prices while growing revenue and profits in the long run. Over the last three years, the company's revenue grew at a rate of 5.3%, while EBITDA increased by 11% and operating margins stayed at 25.48%.

Between 2010 and 2020, Air Products has delivered an annual total return of 17.50%.

Company	APC	LIN
3-year Revenue Growth (%)	5.4	12.3
3-year EBITDA Growth (%)	11	7.2
Current Operating Margin (%)	25.48	13.21
Dividend (%)	1.73	1.47
Average Annual Total Return 2010–2020 (%)	17.50	51.08

Meanwhile, Air Products has a positive economic profit, which means it is creating value as it grows. Additionally, it's beating competitor Linde PLC (LIN), which has a negative economic profit. This means that Air Products is a better bet on atmospheric and specialty gases as the industry grows.

Company	ROIC	WACC	ROIC-WACC (Economic profit)
Air Products	11.43%	5.81%	5.62%
Linde	3.16%	4.05%	-0.89%

There's one more reason to buy Air Products: its large presence in the hydrogen market.

During a conference call hosted by Goldman Sachs last May, Air Products Chairman, President and CEO Seifi Ghasemi said the biggest opportunity for the chemical industry is hydrogen. That market is expected to grow exponentially as governments worldwide step up in the fight against environmental pollution.

"No question about it," he said. "Hydrogen is the future, and the companies that get on top of it now will benefit 10, 15 years from now."

Air Products is the world's largest producer of outsourced hydrogen to oil refineries with an extensive pipeline supply network and world-class customer service. Hydrogen is projected to make up 80% of the company's portfolio by 2035.

Meanwhile, investors can collect the company's dividend, which currently yields 1.73%.

Source: Gurufocus, November 13, 2020.

Application

Uber and Lyft: Can their Problems be Fixed?

Uber Technologies (UBER) and Lyft (LYFT) are great companies, but they have a common problem: a string of money-losing quarters, which extends to well before the pandemic outbreak, and makes them less-than-ideal investments.

Since it went public back in the spring of 2019, Uber's stock has gained a meager 4.64%, while Lyft's stock has gained 2.14%, compared to a whopping 82% gain of NASDAQ.

The Root of the Problem

The root of Uber's and Lyft's problem can be traced to fundamentals, specifically the business model of these two companies. The lack of service differentiation creates zero loyalty among their customers, who frequently switch between the two based on service times. (See Uber stock charts on TipRanks.)

Any car that is used to drive customers is likely to have both a Lyft and an Uber sticker in the window, highlighting the lack of differentiation between their services. (See Lyft stock charts on TipRanks.)

The lack of differentiation brings the two companies into an unwanted situation: price competition.

Economists have a good explanation as to how this happens. While the market for the two rideshare apps could work as a duopoly in theory, it instead works as perfect competition in practice.

That's a market where consumers have perfect information on the quality and the price of services, pitting one seller against another—Uber against Lyft in this case.

The companies have no pricing power, so they earn a "normal" profit in the long run.

Can the Problem be Fixed?

Uber and Lyft have been trying to fix their fundamental problem by investing in drivers and innovation to enhance their value propositions.

Here's a quote from Dara Khosrowshahi, CEO of Uber, following the report of Q2 results.

"In Q2, we invested in recovery by investing in drivers, and we made strong progress, with monthly active drivers and couriers in the US increased by nearly 420,000 from February to July. Our platform is getting stronger each quarter, with consumers who engage with both Mobility and Delivery now generating nearly half of our total company Gross Bookings."

Logan Green, co-founder, and chief executive officer of Lyft, is on the same page. "We had a great quarter. We beat our outlook across every metric, and we have growing momentum. Since our inception, we've worked hard to defy the odds with a deep belief in our mission. We've consistently innovated and made big bets, and this is just the beginning. We want to improve people's lives with the world's best transportation, and we will continue working to deliver on this goal."

Christoph Meyer from the Center of Automotive Research at Stamford sees another way the two companies can fix fundamental problem: personalized pricing. That's a pricing policy wherein the two companies charge riders the maximum price—known in economics as the reservation price—but enable that price to be different for every customer, even as the customers receive an identical good or service.

While companies have caused outrage in the past with surge/prime-time pricing, they hold even greater power going forward," says Meyer. "Having moved to partially mask surge pricing and continuing to collect greater amounts of data on its customers, these transportation companies have the potential to achieve one of economics/business' holy grails: perfect price discrimination."

Will these solutions work? It's still too early to say.

Wall Street Weighs In

Meanwhile, the analyst community is bullish on the shares of the two companies. The 22 Wall Street analysts following Uber Technologies have an average 12-month price target of $68.76, with a high forecast of $81.00 and a low forecast of $81.00. The average Uber price target represents a 58.07% increase from the last price of $43.50.

"Likewise, the 20 analysts following Lyft have a 12-month average Lyft price target of $76.24, with a high forecast of $88.00 and a low forecast of $59.00. The average price target represents a 41.58% change from the last price of $53.85.

Summary and Conclusions

Uber and Lyft are good companies but not sound investments. They create tremendous value for customers, but they don't generate any value for stockholders. The root of this problem is the lack of service differentiation of the two companies' business models, as they engage in price competition.

This situation can change over time, through innovation and the application of personalized pricing. At least that's what the two companies' management and some economists think is the right solution.

Source: TipRanks, August 11, 2021.

Chapter Nine

SUMMARY AND CONCLUSION

As history has confirmed again and again, investing in financial markets is a rewarding, and at the same time, a risky game. For some people, this game is just a game of chance no different than a casino game. For others, investing is a game of intelligence, and winning it takes the knowledge of macroeconomics that provide an understanding of the "big investment context," the regime that determines asset allocation, as discussed in the first volume of the book; and microeconomics provides an understanding of the concepts behind successful strategies and the companies that pursue them:

Economies of Scale

Economies of scale are the cost savings associated with a larger *production* scale (size) of a *certain* product; the larger the production scale, the lower the *per unit* (average) product cost. This means that economies of scale arise on the supply side of the market, on savings from a larger production batch with the same fixed resources, on savings from a better bargaining power with suppliers, on better use of logistics, etc.

Economies of scale are more evident in industries that require large fixed costs, which spread as production size expands, such as the electric industry, which requires large fixed outlays for the building of power generating factories and the wiring of neighborhoods; the cable TV industry, which must also wire the neighborhoods and provide content; the manufacturing industries that require the setting up of assembly lines and large distribution networks; the retailing that requires the leasing of large retail space; and the franchising industry, which requires large expenses in developing the product and business concept.

Economies of Scope and Product Differentiation

Economies of scope are the cost savings associated with the expansion of the product line offered for sale by a corporation; the broader the product line, the higher the total cost savings—and the lower the average cost per product offered. Product differentiation is the churning of different products by the same corporation that cater to different market segments. Economies of scope are more evident in industries that provide a family of products that satisfy similar needs, creating synergies in marketing, distribution, transportation, and transactions. Product differentiation is more evident in technology industries, like consumer electronics. They allow companies to set themselves apart from the competition, improve pricing power and to expand into new markets.

Branding

Branding is the creation of a superior corporate and product image that has both rational and emotional consumer appeal. Branding fuels a strong and steady demand for the product, it strengthens pricing power, and makes it difficult for other companies to imitate and replicate the product. Branding is broadly used in consumer and technology products; it begins with the customer, addressing genuine needs and desires; and requires a great deal of investment in product development, marketing, and customer relations. Branding may not survive in the long-run.

Bundling

Bundling is the packaging of different product characteristics to create unique consumer offerings. Bundling is broadly used in the chemical, telecommunications, and beverage industries to raise revenues by allowing companies to exploit market niches, strengthen pricing power, and improve customer loyalty. Bundling is attained through the setting up of different corporate divisions and subsidiaries that offer complimentary goods and services, and through joint ventures and partnerships. Bundling eventually becomes the target of imitation, and often blindsides companies, missing out on emerging markets and technologies.

Economies of Networking

Economies of networking are the benefits associated with a larger and larger number of people using a certain product; the larger the number of people using the product, the more valuable the product to each user. Economies of networking arise on the demand side of the market and are more evident in information and telecommunications industries. Economies of networking allow companies to quickly reach a critical mass of consumers—the early majority. Attaining economies of networking requires a good knowledge of the different product adoption groups, especially the "early adopters," the link between "innovators" and the "early majority." To take advantage of economies of networking, investors must buy the winner, who takes it all.

Franchising

A franchise is a bottom up organization, a form of collective entrepreneurship that allows its members to share the risks and rewards associated with the discovery and exploitation of new business opportunities. It consists of a "core" and a collection of "peripheral units" standing at the same level, competing and cooperating with each other. A franchise organization allows a network organizations to enjoy a number of distinct advantages. First, it is centralized enough to reap the benefits of economies of scale—the advantages associated with a large organization that pulls together a number of services shared by its members: business mentoring and networking; administrative, legal, and accounting support; marketing and advertisement. Investing in franchising can be very rewarding for investors, especially if it comes in the early stages, as the franchiser expands to prime locations.

Innovation

Innovation is about genuine products, new processes, and new business models that improve consumers' lives. Innovation is a form of entrepreneurship, the "other function" of every business enterprise, and the ultimate source of competitive advantage, especially in the highly competitive and saturated markets. By contrast to other functions of a business enterprise, entrepreneurship cannot be performed simply by hiring entrepreneurs, but is fostered within two sets of institutions that release the individual and collective ingenuity and creativity of the members of corporations. Innovation is pursued with institutions and policies that lower the internal and external boundaries of traditional corporations. Innovation is an expensive and risky strategy—that's why some legendary investors steer away from technology companies.

These concepts are not independent from each other. Scale is often supported and reinforced by branding, while innovation supports and reinforces branding. This means that investors must search for companies that excel in more than one area of microeconomics.

Market Control

Market power is a firm's ability to raise prices without a major impact on sales. Market power arises from market control, the ability of the firm to restrict entry of competitors to offer the same or similar products to consumers.

Application

The Sum of All Advantages: How a Sleeper Stock Has Outperformed Apple

If you have been following Apple's stock closely, you wouldn't expect to find another stock that has outperformed it, not at least among old retailers selling screws and bolts. Yes, screws and bolts, that's what retailer Fastenal Co sells. Since 1987, its stock has outperformed the stocks of Apple and Microsoft—gaining 37,178% compared to Apple's 5,542%, and Microsoft's 9,906%. What is the secret of its success?

Answer: Multiple advantages that constrain entry of new competitors to its business. One of its advantages is **scale**, the cost savings associated with a larger corporate size; Fastenal has 2,585 stores in the U.S. and Mexico. Another advantage is **scope**, the cost savings associated with the offering for sale of different products by a single corporation rather than by different corporations; Fastenal sells hundreds of thousands of MRO, construction and OEM products that extend to 15 product lines. A third advantage is **customization**, the benefits associated with the offering of customer-tailored solutions; Fastenal's manufacturing facilities can tailor its products to different customer needs. A fourth advantage is **bundling**, the packaging of different product characteristics to create unique consumer offerings; Fastenal's extensive store network and highly trained personnel allows the company to bundle products with services. A fifth advantage is **aggregation**, the benefits associated with pulling a large number of orders together; Fastenal helps its customers cut their transaction costs by offering them a one-stop solution to their hardware needs.

Compounding Fastenal's multiple advantages is the integration of its supply chain activities that creates a formidable barrier of entry for new competitors—the company owns manufacturing facilities, a transportation fleet, distribution centers, inventory supply systems, and retailing and sales service facilities.

The bottom line: Don't overlook sleeper stocks, especially if they have multiple sources of sustainable competitive advantage.

Source: *Forbes Magazine*, March 29, 2012.

Appendix

Company Journal

Student Name: _____

Company Name: _____

Industry Name: _____

Week One

	Stock Price	Company News
Monday		
Tuesday		
Wednesday		
Thursday		
Friday		
Saturday		
Sunday		

Company Journal

Student Name: _____

Company Name: _____

Industry Name: _____

Week Two

	Stock Price	Company News
Monday		
Tuesday		
Wednesday		
Thursday		
Friday		
Saturday		
Sunday		

Company Journal

Student Name: _____

Company Name: _____

Industry Name: _____

Week Three

	Stock Price	Company News
Monday		
Tuesday		
Wednesday		
Thursday		
Friday		
Saturday		
Sunday		

Company Journal

Student Name: _____

Company Name: _____

Industry Name: _____

Week Four

	Stock Price	Company News
Monday		
Tuesday		
Wednesday		
Thursday		
Friday		
Saturday		
Sunday		

Company Journal

Student Name: _____

Company Name: _____

Industry Name: _____

Week One

	Stock Price	Company News
Monday		
Tuesday		
Wednesday		
Thursday		
Friday		
Saturday		
Sunday		

Company Journal

Student Name: _____

Company Name: _____

Industry Name: _____

Week One

	Stock Price	Company News
Monday		
Tuesday		
Wednesday		
Thursday		
Friday		
Saturday		
Sunday		

Company Journal

Student Name: _____

Company Name: _____

Industry Name: _____

Week One

	Stock Price	Company News
Monday		
Tuesday		
Wednesday		
Thursday		
Friday		
Saturday		
Sunday		

Company Journal

Student Name: _____

Company Name: _____

Industry Name: _____

Week One

	Stock Price	Company News
Monday		
Tuesday		
Wednesday		
Thursday		
Friday		
Saturday		
Sunday		

Company Journal

Student Name: _____

Company Name: _____

Industry Name: _____

Week One

	Stock Price	Company News
Monday		
Tuesday		
Wednesday		
Thursday		
Friday		
Saturday		
Sunday		

Company Journal

Student Name: _____

Company Name: _____

Industry Name: _____

Week One

	Stock Price	Company News
Monday		
Tuesday		
Wednesday		
Thursday		
Friday		
Saturday		
Sunday		

Company Journal

Student Name: _____

Company Name: _____

Industry Name: _____

Week One

	Stock Price	Company News
Monday		
Tuesday		
Wednesday		
Thursday		
Friday		
Saturday		
Sunday		

Company Journal

Student Name: _____

Company Name: _____

Industry Name: _____

Week One

	Stock Price	Company News
Monday		
Tuesday		
Wednesday		
Thursday		
Friday		
Saturday		
Sunday		

Company Journal

Student Name: _____

Company Name: _____

Industry Name: _____

Week One

	Stock Price	Company News
Monday		
Tuesday		
Wednesday		
Thursday		
Friday		
Saturday		
Sunday		

REVIEW QUESTIONS

1. The difference between winning and losing stocks is in
   a. the choice of the right stockbroker
   b. the soundness or non-soundness of the business strategies of the underlying companies
   c. the understanding of the economic concepts behind these strategies
   d. the size of stockbroker commissions
   e. b and c

2. Sound portfolio management should begin with
   a. analysis of the strategy of the publicly listed companies
   b. the determination of whether listed companies could gain and preserve a competitive edge against their peers
   c. the choice of the right timing
   d. both a and b
   e. both b and c

3. The "efficiency hypothesis theory" school argues that
   a. markets are always efficient
   b. markets always discount public information
   c. stock prices always reflect public information
   d. prospective traders and investors cannot take advantage of stock price moves
   e. all of the above

4. The "technical analysis" school argues that
   a. investors should rely on daily, weekly, monthly, and annual charts of stock prices and trading volumes to identify stock price patterns and trends
   b. investors should rely on a detailed economic analysis of the situation of publicly listed firms

    c. investors should rely on a detailed financial analysis of the situation of the listed firms

    d. all of the above

    e. none of the above

5. The "fundamental analysis" school applies

    a. a set of detailed charts of stock prices and trading volumes to predict the direction of the stock market

    b. a set of detailed economic and financial indicators to separate the winners from the losers

    c. economic and finance to evaluate different stocks

    d. both b and c

    e. both a and b

6. Economic concepts that are dependent on each other

    a. economies of scale supports and reinforce branding

    b. branding supports and reinforces economies of scale

    c. networking supports and reinforces scale

    d. scale supports and reinforces networking

    e. all of the above

7. For intelligent investors, investing is

    a. a game of intelligence

    b. based on the knowledge of economics

    c. good luck

    d. both a and b

    e. both b and c

8. Economies of scale are

    a. the cost savings associated with a larger production scale of a certain product

    b. the cost savings from a smaller production size

    c. more evident in industries that require small start-up costs

    d. more evident in industries that require large fixed costs

    e. both a and d

9. Economies of scale have contributed to the superior stock performance of

   a. General Motors

   b. Kmart

   c. Walmart

   d. AOL Time Warner

   e. all of the above

10. Economics of scope are

   a. the cost savings associated with the expansion of the product line offered for sale by a corporation

   b. the cost savings associated with the narrowing of the product line offered for sale by corporation

   c. more evident in pharmaceutical distribution and book publishing

   d. less evident in pharmaceutical distribution and book publishing

   e. both a and c

11. Branding

   a. is the creation of a superior corporate and product image that has both rational and emotional consumer appeal

   b. is broadly used in consumer and technology products; it begins with the customer, addressing genuine needs and desires

   c. requires a great deal of investment in product development, marketing, and customer relations

   d. all of the above

   e. none of the above

12. Bundling is

   a. the packaging of different product characteristics to create unique consumer offerings

   b. broadly used in the chemical, telecommunications, and beverage industries to raise revenue

   c. attained through the setting up of different corporate divisions and subsidiaries that offer complimentary goods and services

   d. all of the above

   e. none of the above

13. Economies of networking

   a. are the benefits associated with a larger and larger number of people using a certain product

   b. arise on the demand side of the market

   c. are more evident in information and telecommunications industries

   d. are a fast way reach a critical mass of consumers

   e. all of the above

14. Economies of networking contributed to the superior performance of

   a. Microsoft Corporations

   b. eBay

   c. Ford Corporation

   d. General Motors Corporation

   e. both a and b

15. A franchise is

   a. a bottom up organization

   b. a form of collective entrepreneurship that allows its members to share the risks and rewards associated with the discovery and exploitation of new business opportunities

   c. consists of a "core" and a collection of "peripheral units" standing at the same level, competing and cooperating with each other

   d. a source of sustainable competitive advantage

   e. all of the above

16. Innovation is

   a. about genuine products, new processes, and new business models that improve consumers' lives

   b. a form on entrepreneurship, the "other function" of every business enterprise

   c. the ultimate source of competitive advantage, especially in the highly competitive and saturated markets

   d. an expensive and risky strategy

   e. all of the above

17. Innovation has contributed to the success of

    a. Starbucks

    b. Apple

    c. American International Group

    d. a and b only

    e. b and c only

18. Product differentiation is

    a. the marginal altering of product offerings

    b. the radical altering of product offerings

    c. the packaging of different products

    d. the discounting of different products

    e. all of the above

19. Bundling has contributed to the success of

    a. Walmart

    b. Yum! Brands

    c. Microsoft

    d. all of the above

    e. b and c only

20. Branding has contributed to the success of

    a. Walmart

    b. Kmart

    c. Nike

    d. all of the above

    e. none of the above

ANSWER KEY

1. E
2. D
3. E
4. A
5. D
6. E
7. D
8. E
9. C
10. E
11. D
12. D
13. E
14. E
15. E
16. E
17. D
18. A
19. E
20. C

BIBLIOGRAPHY

Adams, G. *The E-Business Revolution and The New Economy*. Mason, OH: SouthWestern. 2004.

Berman, K. D. "Innovation Outpaced the Marketplace." *The Wall Street Journal*, Sept. 26, 2002, B1 and B8.

Blackshaw, Pete. *Satisfied Customers Tell Three Friends, Angry Customers Tell 3,000: Running a Business in Today's Consumer-Driven World*. New York: Doubleday. 2008.

Braun, N. "Individual Thresholds and Social Diffusion." *Rationality and Society*, Vol. 7, No. 2, 167–182, 1995.

Brock, W. A., and S. N. Durlauf. "Discrete Choice with Social Interaction." *Review of Economic Studies* Vol. 68, 235–260, 1997.

Caulfield, Brian. "Saving $3 billion the HP Way." *Business 2.0*, May 2003, 52–54.

Christensen, C., and Rayner, M. *The Innovator's Solution*. Cambridge, MA: Harvard Business School Press. 2003.

Cross, R., Liedtka, J., and Weiss, L. "A Practical Guide to Social Networks." *Harvard Business Review* Vol 83(3).

Fishman, Charles. "Why We Buy." *Fat Company*, Issue 99, November 1999.

Floortje, Alkemade, and Carolina Castaldi. "Strategies for the Diffusion of Innovations on Social Networks." *Computational Economics* Vol. 25, 3–23, 2005.

Gladwell, Malcolm. *The Tipping Point*. New York: Back Bay Books. 2005.

Gloor, P., and Scott M. Cooper. *Cool Hunting: Chasing Down the Next Big Thing*. New York: AMACOM, 2007.

Grönroos, C. "A Service Quality Model and Its Marketing Implications." *European Journal of Marketing* Vol. 18, No. 4, 36–44, 1984.

Godes, D., D. Mayzlin, Y. Chen; S. Das, C. Dellarocas, B. Pfeiffer, B. Libai, S. Sen, M. Shi, and P. Verlegh. "The Firm's Management of Social Interactions." *Marketing Letters* Vol. 16, Nos. 3/4, 415–428, 2005.

Godin, S. "Your Product, Your Customer." *Forbes*, May 7, 2007.

Leibenstein, H. "Bandwagon, Snob and Veblen Effects in the Theory of Consumers' Demand." *Quarterly Journal of Economics* Vol. 64, 183–207, 1950.

Livingston, S. "Blog Buzz Helps Companies Catch Trends in the Making." *Washington Post*, March 3, 2006, A01.

Markides, C., and Geroski, P. "The Innovator's Prescription: The Art of Scale." *Business and Strategy*, Summer 2004.

Mossberg, W. "Beautiful but Too Big? New Apple Power Book Boasts 17-Inch Screen." *The Wall Street Journal*, April 3, 2003.

Mourdoukoutas, P. *Business Strategy in a Semiglobal Economy*. New York: Sharpe, Inc. 2006.

Mourdoukoutas, P., and Siomkos, G. *Crossing the Tipping Point: WOM and Buzz Marketing*. Springer, 2009.

Mourdoukoutas, P., and Papadimitriou, S. *Nurturing Entrepreneurship in a Globalizing Economy: Institutions and Policies*. Westport, CT: Quorum Books. 2002.

Mourdoukoutas, P. *The Global Corporation: The Decolonization of International Business*. Westport, CT: Quorum Books. 1999.

Mourdoukoutas, P. *Collective Entrepreneurship in a Globalizing Economy*. Westport, CT: Quorum Books. 1999.

Mussa, M. "Factors Driving Global Economic Integration." http://www.imf.org/external/speeches/2000/082500.htm.

Schelling, Thomas C. *Micromotives and Macrobehavior*. New York: W. W. Norton & Company. 1978.

Schultz, H., and D. J. Yang. *Pour Your Heart Into It*. New York: Hyperion. 1997.

Tapscott, D., and A. Williams. *Wikinomics: How Mass Collaboration Changes Everything*. New York: Portfolio. 2006.

Tedeschi, B. "Online Sellers Discover The Power of Video Clips." *The New York Times,* February 5, 2007.

Vranica, Suzanne. "McDonald's Tries for 'Viral' Buzz: Web Auction of French Fry That Resembles Lincoln Aims to Corral Young Men." *The Wall Street Journal*, February 1, 2005.

ABOUT THE AUTHOR

Panos Mourdoukoutas, PhD is Chair of the Department of Economics at Long Island University. He is the author of more than forty articles published in professional journals and magazines, including the *New York Times, Barron's, Japan Times, Edge Singapore,* and *European Business Review.*

Dr. Mourdoukoutas is also the author or co-author of fifteen books, including *Japan's Emerging New Economy: Opportunity and Strategy in World Business* (Thomson/South-Western), *Business Strategy in a Semiglobal Economy* (M. E. Sharpe, Inc.), and the *Ten Golden Rules* (Hampton Roads Publishing).